NEPHILIM NIGHTMARE

Fred DeRuvo

Published in Scotts Valley, California, by Study-Grow-Know
www.studygrowknow.com • www.rightly-dividing.com • www.adroitpublications.com

Scripture quotations unless otherwise noted, are from The Holy Bible, King James Version. This version is in the public domain.

Cover Design: Fred DeRuvo

Library of Congress Cataloging-in-Publication Data

DeRuvo, Fred, 1957 –

ISBN 0982644329
EAN-13 9780982644324

1. Religion – Demonology & Satanism

Contents

For such are false apostles, deceitful workers, transforming themselves into the apostles of Christ. And no marvel; for Satan himself is transformed into an angel of light. Therefore it is no great thing if his ministers also be transformed as the ministers of righteousness; whose end shall be according to their works.

– 2 Corinthians 11:13-15 (KJV)

FOREWORD

Something tends to stand out among the volumes of research available regarding the subject of the New Age. It is the fact that many who are seriously involved in this movement have some type of religious training in their backgrounds. What I mean by that is that many individuals come from households where some type of religion was practiced, or was at least acknowledged in some way.

In any number of cases, each parent had their own particular religious background, though the child may have grown up ultimately practicing nothing. For instance, it is interesting to note that many come from Baptist backgrounds, Jewish backgrounds, other protestant affiliations, along with various religions and of course, many are atheists or agnostics.

One individual I came across in my research is Lia Shapiro, and she is one who comes from a mixed culture/religion. Her father was Jewish (though a professed atheist), while Lia's mother was Southern Baptist. In her book *Comes the Awakening : Realizing the Divine Nature of Who You Are (A Pleiadian Book)* she gives a bit of her testimony, so to speak. It's an interesting, albeit sad one. For her, it was a mixed bag of outlooks on life. She herself states, "*My parents never did figure out what beliefs or religion we should be raised with.*"[1]

She readily admits that while she grew, no religion was practiced in their home and while she also admits to not knowing a thing about the Bible, she grew up learning to trust in her own spiritual power. As an adult, she now states that she is a higher level Pleiadian. Through a blended path of learning the hippie ways, to giving peace a chance, to protesting, to a time of spiritual awakening, Lia came to

---

[1] Lia Shapiro *Comes the Awakening : Realizing the Divine Nature of Who You Are* (Star Street Press: Washington DC, 2000), 9

learn that she was actually not a physical being with a spirit, but actually a spiritual being, with a body of flesh.

These realizations came to her over time, and through visions that she encountered. It was through these visions that she came to know herself and her purpose. Within those visions, she met an individual whom she describes as a *light being*. This particular light being turned out to be none other than Jesus. Of course, as she quickly discovered, this Jesus was not the Jesus that *"the Bible has made of Him, but he was as we are."*[2]

Like many, Lia came to the realization that she is God (she uses the capital "g"). She describes an experience that she states was being *born again*, though at the time was not aware of what that term meant. It was a day in which she says she came to God, but not through Jesus. Of that experience, she states, *"I didn't believe in Jesus or not in the Biblical sense anyway. I didn't believe in sin either, but I read the prayer in the booklet my sister had sent just in case. That was the day I simply gave up. I said, 'Okay, God, I give up,' and I read the prayer twice just to make sure. I had no one to turn to but God, although I was not sure where God was; I only knew that I needed divine help."*[3]

Experiences like those just described are fast becoming the norm for people involved with the New Age. The New Age is vastly more than simply people meditating to achieve various stages of relaxation. It incorporates a complex belief-system, in which Nephilim demons masquerade as aliens to teach human beings the "truth" of the Bible and all about God.

If you read my last book, *Demons in Disguise*, then you are already aware of my perspective, with respect to demons and Nephilim. You

---

[2] Lia Shapiro *Comes the Awakening : Realizing the Divine Nature of Who You Are* (Star Street Press: Washington DC, 2000), 12

[3] Ibid, 14

know that I believe that the demons of Christ's day *and* of our day are largely the *Nephilim*, who were forced to vacate their physical bodies when the global Flood of Noah's day came upon the entire earth. Since that time, they roam the spiritual realm and our physical realm seeking another body to inhabit and control.

One of the greatest weapons of deceit that these Nephilim demons use against human beings besides our lack of knowledge is our *gullibility*. Because we are fallen creatures, everything about us is fallen, including our *emotions*.

These Nephilim demons have learned that they can control us through our *emotions*. We are susceptible to their *suggestions*, their *false visions* (more properly termed *hallucinations*), and more because these things *affect* our *emotions*. Once they have our emotions, they have us.

To those who are *not* looking for any type of spiritual utopia, these people are theirs already as well. These individuals, unlike those within aspects of the New Age movement, believe in themselves just like New Agers do, but their reasoning is built on the axiom, "you gotta watch out for number one." In truth, *both* groups cater to this axiom. While the person normally seen as the outcast of society, often found within the repugnant underbelly, tends to live by this adage that points the focus directly on them and their needs, the New Agers' motivation is no different. It only *appears* to be different, since what they *seem* to be yearning for is much more altruistic. The truth of the matter is that *all* groups within society not authentically Christian yearn to fulfill their own selfish desires anyway they can. To believe that because of involvement in the New Age, the motivation becomes instantly the opposite of self-serving is merely part of the enemy's deception.

This book is the result of studying and researching aspects of the New Age that I had only heard of, but not deeply. The amount of lies that are routinely spoken to human beings, as well as the twisted way in which the Bible is regularly taught by these same Nephilim demons is astounding. The most tragic aspect of all of this is that these individuals who have fallen so hard under the spell of the Nephilim hoard, that they roundly and without hesitation reject what the Bible teaches, believing it to be *false*. They prefer to receive and accept the words of a strange being who neither is asked to prove his identity, nor offers to do so.

Of course, it does not necessarily connect only to the New Age movement throughout the world. These Nephilim demons and fallen angels are also busy plying their lies and deceptions onto the visible Church. They do this through people who *sound* (and *are*) very intelligent. In many cases, they have a very easy going writing style, which tends to draw the reader into their snare. Many are completely unaware that these individuals are foisting absolute heresy onto the individuals within the visible Church and they are able to do this because most people do not know what they believe.

The Pleiadian web of deceit is really the Nephilim web of deceit, for it is through these beings that the lie is being perpetrated today; as Pleiadians for the New Age and Aquarian movements, and as Christian-looking leaders who, while using terminology familiar with the average Christian, undergirds their message with blasphemous views. When Christians come out *against* their views, these same Christian-looking leaders have no difficulty in remonstrating against them in order to embarrass them into silence. It is quite an intricate web that Nephilim demons and fallen angels have worked to create over centuries. Largely, humanity is certainly caught within the many layers of this web. They have been busy spinning their web, slowing, methodically, and consistently wrapping it around anyone who comes too close.

Extrication from this web seems impossible, because there are too many voices out there preaching the same message, though unique to various groups. However, God is able. He calls us to never forget the command that we received from our Lord Jesus Christ, who stated that we were to evangelize the lost.

Fellow Christian, these people are the mission field. They need Christ and the salvation that only He offers. Many of these people may be well be beyond the ability to be saved, yet neither our prayers, nor our evangelism of them should cease. Whether they can be, will be, or are beyond the ability to be saved is not ours to judge.

As you read this book, may God grant you His heart, His compassion, His wisdom, and His words to reach out to people like Lia, people who are in desperate need of His truth and His salvation.

Fred DeRuvo, April 2010

Chapter 1
Dream Weavers

As far as I'm concerned, the *Nephilim Nightmare* is exactly that; a *nightmare* being perpetrated against humanity and building to its scheduled and foreordained climax. It goes much further than just the New Age, or the space alien phenomenon. In fact, I believe it has wormed its way into virtually every area of society, though in many ways, people seem to be unaware. This goes along perfectly with the delusion that God says He is sending people so that they will believe *the* lie (cf. 2 Thessalonians 2:11). People are *not* merely focusing primarily on *aliens*, or space beings, or whatever label they are given, yet that seems to be the most obvious channel.

Folks the world over have been and continue to be *affected* and *infected* with the unadulterated evil that Nephilim demons foist upon them as they search for available human *hosts*. What is fascinating *and* alarming is the way in which this has occurred, slowly and consistently over time. It makes sense that they would opt to work their program in such a way, so that people do not become wise to their true purpose and threat. Beyond this, the space alien connection as revealed to the world through the New Age is simply *part* of the problem. A problem far more nuanced and *seemingly* less evil than other avenues through which Nephilim demons, fallen angels, and even Satan himself have infiltrated earthly society.

Not a Pretty Subject

Parts of this book are not "pretty," though it has a wonderful and bright conclusion, for those who trust in Christ. These pages endeavor to reveal the work of evil spirits masquerade who masquerade as *Pleiadians*.

Beyond this, we delve into the *underbelly* of society, into areas not normally noticed by the average individual, areas in which these same groups of evil spirits (Nephilim demons and fallen angels), either masquerade as something else entirely, or choose to remain deep in the shadows, well *behind* the human being they have infected with their diabolical and detrimental "theology."

In noting this, please understand that it is *not* the intent of this book to glorify the violence, depravity, or rank evil of human beings who have given themselves over to these spiritual entities, either knowingly or unknowingly. The majority of details in most cases that are highlighted within these pages are purposefully kept to a minimum. Yet, at the same time, these areas need highlighting so that it is understood with what we are dealing.

The spiritual beings that flit from their dimension to ours instantly and disappear just as quickly are without question, *malevolent.* Even atheists and agnostics who have spent years researching the alien phenomenon have arrived at the same conclusion though they may not believe in demons and fallen angels. These same entities that wreaked havoc on God's Creation to the point that God had to destroy it, save Noah, his family and the animals they took with them on the Ark, are with us today.

These beings, while their physical bodies may have *died* at one point in time, in spiritual form have continued to chase after human flesh, incarcerating themselves within the human body whenever possible. This gives them the ability to do *more* than they would if they merely remained in the shadows of the spiritual dimension apart from flesh.

By bringing themselves in contact with, and eventually taking up residence within human beings, they once again experience what they experienced during the days of Noah, when they enjoyed the physical experience their original bodies afforded them. The physical pleasures these beings chase after are assuaged *only* when they have another physical body to work through and manipulate.

Since the time God saw fit to destroy His entire living Creation, these Nephilim demons, fallen angels, and Satan himself know that they roam on *borrowed* time. They realize their end is sure, simply because of the fact that Christ died and *was resurrected.* The death of Christ made the victory possible and the resurrection *sealed* the deal. Neither Death nor Satan could hold the Author of Life in the ground. Certainly as the book of Job testifies, they have always been under God's control.

Satan was actually defeated from the moment God issued the prophecy of his coming defeat through the Messiah's death, in Genesis 3. This prophetic utterance by God sealed the deal *then*; however, Satan has continued to work since then because in keeping with his natural proclivities, he desires to overturn God's work and His promises. God has put off Satan'sactual sentencing until His full purposes are met.

Satan has yet to succeed. His record of accomplishment regarding the dismantling God's will and purposes amounts to a big, fat *zero*. Satan has done *nothing* to change God's intended direction and in every way, has helped in bringing God's will to fruition. This assures us that he will *never* succeed in changing the intended direction of any of God's purposes. Yet he continues to try. What else does he have? Redemption for him and his angels (along with the Nephilim demons) is out of the question. It is impossible because that option does not exist. He lives with that fact and because of it, tries desperately with all that he has to circumvent God's perfect will. However, *trying* is not *winning*.

Spiritual Beings in the Spiritual Realms

One of the biggest problems facing the world today is something that most are not even aware exists. Spiritual beings roam this earth constantly looking around for people with whom they can *infect* and *affect* with their malevolence.

The New Age/Space Alien phenomenon is something that presents fallen angels, demons, and Satan in a light that is *acceptable* to many people. It presents them as *good*, with *altruistic* motives. They come to help. They remain in the shadows for the most part, because they do not want to *scare* the world's population. They allegedly endeavor to bring us up to speed over time, as gently as possible. They have only our best interests at heart. In fact, nearly everything they present about themselves is designed to make them appear non-threatening and philanthropic.

However, the New Age/Space Alien situation is only *one* of the avenues through which they have revealed themselves and through which they work. In many ways, this is by far the most important channel, because it is through the New Age movement that the coming Antichrist will likely receive his greatest endorsement. In fact, in all likelihood, the one-world government *and* one-world religion may very well be introduced to the world through the New Age movement.

In what other areas have these malevolent beings worked and continue to work? How are they getting either their message out, or simply bringing an increase of violence to this world? There are in fact, many ways. We will certainly spend time dealing with the New Age/Space alien connection, but we cannot ignore the other areas that have been utilized to bring change to this planet.

It is extremely important to realize that Satan has *not* placed all of his eggs in one basket, yet all those various eggs ultimately point to the same purpose (and will come to the same end). Just as he is multi-faceted in many respects, he brings his purposes to bear on a situation as is best suited for the individuals with whom he is dealing at that time.

We must take the time to investigate these areas in order to know just how deeply these sentient beings have permeated society. As stated, it does not paint a pretty picture, yet it is a picture with which we must all become familiar.

Chapter 2

Underworld

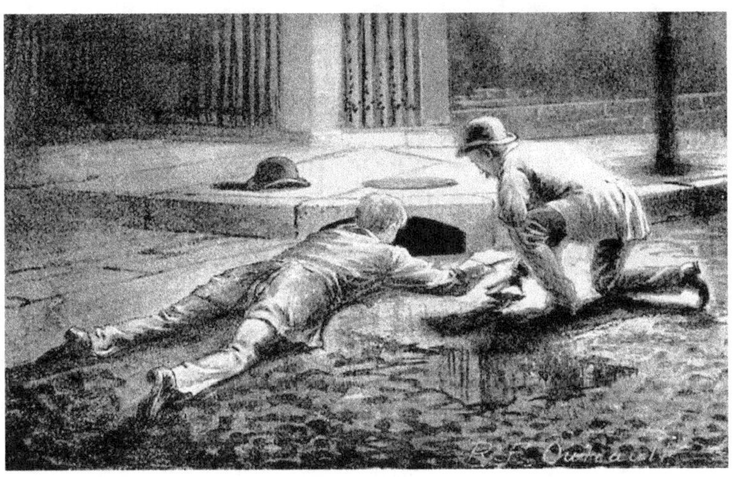

It is easy to go through life not really noticing all the evil. That may appear to be an inaccurate statement, yet it is true. After all, who really wants to spend time researching just how bad human beings have become? Who wants to know that the depravity of man has reached such a low point that it has today? If you are not in the crime unit of a police department, then you really do not have to focus on it.

However, if we avoid this knowledge, then we avoid seeing the world for what it is, and if we avoid seeing the world for what it is, we fail to understand just how short the time is for multitudes of people on this planet to make a decision *for* Christ and His salvation. While it is relatively easy to become preoccupied with the many things in this life, such as our pension plans, a bigger house, or a better car, the Lord would have us concentrate on our *roots*. Our roots lie *in* Him, because as Paul tells us in Romans 6, we died in Christ and we are no longer slaves to sin. In Romans 7, he affirms that we are no longer under the Law. In this same chapter, he points out that it is *because* we are free *from the tyranny* of the Law, Christ has actually *fettered* us to Him! We are *not* free to simply live a life of grandiose relaxation, counting the days until we retire so that we can begin drawing on that pension that we've spent years building up.

We have been released from the dictates of the Law, in order that we might *bear fruit unto righteousness*. This will only happen as we abide in Christ and this is one of the unique privileges of being authentic believers.

Seared Consciences

At the extreme opposite end of the spectrum are those who not only do *not* know Christ as Savior and Lord, but have also gotten to the point where their consciences are seared. Because of this, it becomes tempting to see these individuals as *beyond* salvation's ability to save them. While we cannot, nor should not judge their spiritual condition, it is just as important to understand that the individuals, who seem so far away from God, are likely seated deeply in the very middle of the enemy's camp. This knowledge should support Paul's teaching that we war *not* against flesh and blood, but against those beings in the spiritual realms. It is easy to forget that truth and focus on the *person* instead.

The truth of the matter is that these individuals, in many respects, have become living repositories for fallen angels and Nephilim demons. We are aware of what Paul tells Timothy about the last days and how bad people would become (cf. 2 Timothy 2). Paul also told the Thessalonians that lawlessness (which he called "secret") is already at work in his life since his day! (cf. 2 Thessalonians 2) If this is so, then how much more ground has lawlessness gained since Paul?

In speaking of the End Times, Jesus stated, *"And because iniquity shall abound, the love of many shall wax cold,"* (Matthew 24:12). Even many professing Christians today take a *laissez-faire* approach to sin. We excuse ourselves because we are "only" human. We believe that since God forgives, then *when* we sin, His forgiveness is *there*. This may be true (that His forgiveness extends to all my future sins, yet this does not give me a license to sin!). God is often seen as the doting grandfather who cannot love his grandchildren enough, winks at sin and readily overlooks all the things that offend Him. This position is thoroughly unbiblical.

The problem of course is that we are *not* to continue in a *lifestyle* of sinning *after* we become Christians. This is not to say that we will be free from all sin for the remainder of our lives. It means that we should learn to *hate* sin as much as God does, endeavoring to submit ourselves to Him in order that by His strength, we can overcome the temptation to sin in our daily lives.

The second epistle of Peter chapter two paints a picture of imposters who call themselves followers of God, yet live the way they want to live, telling people what they want to hear. These people have been around seemingly forever and will be around until the end.

Satan is Working In and Through People

Currently, we rarely read about how Satan is working through those in our society who have fallen so low, that to them, evil is good, or even *funny*. Yet, these people exist.

Recently I was researching in books and on the Internet and came across a website that updates weekly (if not daily). There before me, were the crime files of people who have participated in some of the most nauseating cases of cruelty known to humankind!

It is not even so much that some of these people are *murderers* or *rapists*. Certainly, this is terrible and bad enough, but most of these individuals do not stop there. One man decided he needed to teach his mother a lesson, and did so by hogtying her then proceeded to beat her with a hammer and stomp her chest. She finally managed to escape and entered the hospital in critical condition with a fractured skull as well as severe bruising on her chest and elsewhere.

Another individual decided that she found a novel way to kill a kitten and did so. I wish I could say it was quick, but that would be asking too much. After she had done the terrible deed, she bragged and joked about it to her friends.

Another woman decided that her 3-year old needed to learn a valuable lesson, so she drove her to the city in the middle of the night and left her on a street corner. Others beat their toddlers or small children to death. Still others molested *infants* and *then* beat them to death. Folks, this is demonic activity because human beings by themselves do not live like this. This is not to say that the human being is free from blame. They are fully culpable, but to be clear, the enemy of our souls is clearly working in and through them.

To look at the mug shots of these people says only one thing. Their pictures seem to scream that they are at the very least, *oppressed* by Nephilim demons. Many are likely *possessed* by them. Normal human beings do not act this way, because we have a conscience. While it is true that humans can force their consciences to stop issuing warnings so that it stops telling them when they are doing something wrong, I believe that this happens primarily in collusion with spiritual entities.

The spiritual beings that yearn to take up residence in another body of flesh *need* to exist in that body, without worrying about the constant remonstrations of conscience. It will not do to have their human host doing what they can do to expel the unwanted spiritual *leech*.

Over time, these malicious spiritual beings continue to override the conscience until it stops speaking its warnings and eventually goes silent. From this point on, the people who have been literally *infested* with numerous beings from the spiritual realm live in such a way that those spirits living within them have their way. They do what *they* want to do, using that particular human body as if it was their own. The Nephilim demons have successfully supplanted the conscience and human will by overpowering it into silence.

Think about people like this. We have all read about them in the newspapers, or seen them on the TV news programs. They seem to have absolutely no remorse or even feeling for any of their crimes when finally brought to justice. They defy description in many cases.

There they sit in the courtroom, as stoic as a brick wall, showing no emotion, sitting through the proceedings as if they are having lunch at some diner. It simply does not seem to matter to them at all. They did what they did and that is all there is to it. It is too bad that they were caught, but that certainly does not bother the Nephilim demons that reside within them. When the person goes to jail, they go with them. If the person is eventually executed, or killed in prison, these same Nephilim demons find another body to reside in, and then it begins all over.

Space Beings are Only *Part* of the Problem

It seems that many people are focusing on today's space aliens to the extent that much of the evil in the world is not noticed. We generally do not give it too much notice because underneath, we believe that evil has always been and will always be with us, until the Lord puts an everlasting end to it.

The trouble is that when the Lord spoke of the *Last Days* and His eventual *return*, He specifically pointed to two periods in history, in which both cases had an *overabundance* or *unnatural* amount of *evil*. While focusing on the space alien connection is *important* (and we will get to it), it is equally important to understand how much evil these Nephilim beings are able to create within society.

As just mentioned, we have heard of, or read about murderers who stand before a judge in a courtroom with no seeming conscience. They sit there, seemingly nonplussed over their situation and potential sentencing. It is as if they are watching a TV show simply to pass the time, not because they are interested in watching the TV show, but because they have nothing better to do.

Jeffrey Dahmer, John Wayne Gacy, and a host of other self-indulgent human beings at one point in time, likely gave themselves over to the enemy (whether they knew it or not). Since that time, their lives slowly and deliberately *became* the life of the entity(ies) within them. Eventually, they simply did the bidding of those spiritual beings, having nearly become one with them. While the real Jeffrey Dahmer was locked away somewhere deep in the recesses of his own body, he either felt he had no ability to get past these demons, or cared not to, committing himself to whatever fate they created for him.

In researching Dahmer's case, it becomes clear that he at least was likely *possessed*. One of Dahmer's last victims who managed to escape his clutches said that as they sat there in Dahmer's living room watching "The Exorcist," Dahmer began to *crow* loudly like a chicken, flapping his arms. As the man looked at Dahmer's face, he could see that it was as if Dahmer was not there. It was surely Dahmer's physical face, but it was most certainly *not* Dahmer's personality.

The man tried to leave and instantly, Dahmer overtook him wrestling him to the floor. The man said later that he could not believe the amount of strength Dahmer exhibited as he struggled to free himself! Eventually, the man *was* able to escape, running all the way to the police station. It was at that point that things completely fell apart for Dahmer. When the police arrived, they found a docile, non-combative man who was easily taken into custody after the police discovered body parts in the refrigerator and elsewhere.

This same Dahmer sat in the courtroom day after day, while the evidence piled up. Dahmer was a sick man, *exceedingly* sick. It simply cannot be described here, but human beings do not do the things that Dahmer did *after* he killed someone, much less regarding the fact that he killed repeatedly, one victim after another. Those actions are from Nephilim demons and fallen angels of the spiritual realm. Yet, Dahmer is still culpable as far as God is concerned.

John Wayne Gacy is another individual whom we all know of, and of whom we would likely have never guessed that he was what he was underneath his clown costume and his outwardly friendly demeanor. This was a man loved by people, including his neighbors. He held friendly and fun block parties. He even shook hands with the president at the time! No one then had a clue to his aberrant lifestyle, which unleashed the demons within him.

Eventually, the net began to close around Gacy, as police began to focus on him. One detective, while inside Gacy's house took a moment to use the bathroom. While there, he later said he noticed the most putrid odor. It was abnormal.

Finally, Gacy's hidden and horrific lifestyle was unmasked and the world went "Huh?" because no one would have guessed that he had done what it appeared that he had done. Whenever one of these individuals is unmasked, many others go unnoticed.

The truth of the matter that it appears as though there are groups of Nephilim demons who concentrate on imposing their will on human beings, either through outward oppression, or inward possession. Other spiritual beings masquerade as types of visitors from space. Others remain in the shadows, likely helping Satan directly with his plans to rule (and enslave) the world.

In other words, the first two groups of beings keep humanity preoccupied, either with fear through crime, or interest and/or fear of the alien phenomenon. This preoccupation allows them to use the same sleight of hand that a master magician uses while performing his tricks.

Superb Magician

Silvia and I, while dining at a restaurant one evening, noticed a magician going from table to table. He had been hired by the restaurant to entertain people quietly while they waited for their dinner to be served to them.

While he did not use the normal flourish of the most stage magicians, his tricks were nonetheless, quite impressive, and all done with merely a few coins. He would place a coin on the table for us to look at and then with both hands in full view, made the coin disappear and reappear somewhere else.

I tend to pride myself on figuring out many illusions. Some of course slip by me completely, as did this magician's. For the life of me, I could not figure out how he did what he did! He was very good and smooth. Though his hands were not more than two feet from our faces, we could see *nothing* that gave away the trick.

As we left the restaurant that evening, we were still marveling at his prestidigitation. As we walked to our car, we must have passed his (due to the license plate, which had something to do with magic), and I immediately noticed that his car was very expensive. Obviously, this magician was extremely good at what he did and this little stint at the restaurant tonight was probably a very small part of the overall places he plied his trade.

This is what Nephilim demons and fallen angels do. They are so good at it, that gullible humans simply *believe* them. They do so because they see no flaw in their presentation and because of that, they are impressed into believing what they see and hear is the truth. They believe that what those beings are saying or showing them *must* be true because there was nothing that gave them away.

Satan of course, does not deliberately leave anything to chance. He is doing his best to cover all of his bases. We know the end of the story though because it has already been written, and authentic believers are the benefactors.

Because of *all* that is going on in our society today, it is necessary to realize that we will see *more evil* as time goes by, just as we will witness more *signs in the heavens*. People's moral fiber will continue to deteriorate on a massive scale as Nephilim demons turn up the heat. More encounters with aliens will be seen and experienced as well.

All of these things serve to create a complete societal *disillusionment* with the world, as it currently exists. People are afraid of the increasing evil. They are afraid that we will use up the earth's resources. They fear the possibility of more wars, and they are in general, fearful for their future.

Groups of Nephilim demons and fallen angels have worked both ends against the middle – one group working through *direct* evil with the other working through *alien* phenomenon and *New Age* thought. An offshoot of this New Age thought is becoming steadily more influential within the visible Church, in spite of the fact that many deny this reality. A situation has come into existence, which is

Evil Beings: Working Both Ends Against the Middle
©2010 F. DERUVO
In the Skies
ROSWELL
On the Ground
FRESH TURKEYS
CEMENT

pushing people toward an expectancy that they believe will only find fulfillment in the coming of *one individual* who will be able to solve the problems of the world.

It is all coming to a head. Just as people got so caught up in thinking that President Obama was the voice of *change and hope*, and many even viewed him as a type of Messiah, it was only a warm-up for the final man who will be seen as the Messiah because of what he will be able to accomplish. Instead of this expectancy being relegated to the United States and a few foreign countries where Obama was concerned, the excitement and hope for this last coming ruler will reach a fevered pitch worldwide. The mob mentality will usher him into his foreordained position as ruler of the world.

This may be difficult for some to appreciate; another one-world ruler. That seems far-fetched and an impossibility, yet it will happen.

Chapter 3

Love Bites

It has been impossible to miss the fact that within society today, vampires have become a very real subject to many. By that I mean, that the vampire phenomenon has literally taken the world by storm. It truly seems that people cannot get enough and some of the most recent visions of these entities prove that fact.

Twilight is a case in point. This vampire story began on the small screen and quickly segued to the silver screen. Created by Stephanie Meyer, the story is about an unorthodox vampire who meets the girl he believes to be his soul mate. "Bella *Swan has always been a little bit different. Never one to run with the crowd, Bella never cared about*

fitting in with the trendy, plastic girls at her Phoenix, Arizona high school. When her mother remarried and Bella chooses to live with her father in the rainy little town of Forks, Washington, she didn't expect much of anything to change. But things do change when she meets the mysterious and dazzlingly beautiful Edward Cullen. For Edward is nothing like any boy she's ever met. He's nothing like anyone she's ever met, period. He's intelligent and witty, and he seems to see straight into her soul. In no time at all, they are swept up in a passionate and decidedly unorthodox romance - unorthodox because Edward really isn't like the other boys. He can run faster than a mountain lion. He can stop a moving car with his bare hands. Oh, and he hasn't aged since 1918. Like all vampires, he's immortal. That's right - vampire. But he doesn't have fangs - that's just in the movies. And he doesn't drink human blood, though Edward and his family are unique among vampires in that lifestyle choice."[4]

Vampires have come a long way since I was a kid. In fact, by the time I was old enough to watch movies and understand them, the classic

[4] http://www.imdb.com/title/tt1099212/

monsters of Universal Studios had already been on film for over 30 years, yet they were making a comeback to my generation of kids who had become interested in monsters like Dracula, Wolfman, Frankenstein and the rest.

Classic vs. Modern Monsters

However, it should be noted that these classic monsters were *mild* compared to the monsters of today. Then, they were obviously evil, no questions asked. Since then they have literally morphed into much more than monster and something far closer to being a type of *god*. Lines between good and evil have evaporated. The vampires, lycanthropes, and other monsters of today are far more powerful, much more attractive, and seemingly unstoppable than were the monsters of yesteryear.

Lon Chaney's *Wolman*, Boris Karloff's *Frankenstein*, and Bela Lugosi's *Dracula* were all scary. They also had very clear *limitations*. The one major thing that separated the monsters of that era from those of today is the *supernatural* connection. While we knew that changing from a human to a bat *was* supernatural, it was not dwelt on, nor was it glorified.

Today's monsters are also supernatural and that connection *is* glorified. In fact, the supernatural connection has become the primary focus in most of these envisionings. The Twilight franchise is simply one case in point.

Apparently, the creator of the series – Stephanie Meyer – is Mormon and sees a direct connection between vampires, their desire for blood, and Christianity. She recalls how she came up with the concept of Twilight. *"I woke up (on that June 2nd) from a very vivid dream. In my dream, two people were having an intense conversation in a meadow in the woods. One of these people was just your average girl. The other person was fantastically beautiful, sparkly, and a vampire. They were discussing the difficulties inherent in the facts that*

A) they were falling in love with each other while B) the vampire was particularly attracted to the scent of her blood, and was having a difficult time restraining himself from killing her immediately."[5]

Meyer has been written about in Time magazine, as well as in other magazines and Internet articles. Overnight, she has become another J. K. Rowling of Harry Potter fame. She states, *"in the course of six months, Twilight was dreamed, written, and accepted for publication."*[6]

I have always thought it odd that Harry Potter became an obsession literally overnight. Both Meyer and J. K. Rowling came out of nowhere and both became instant celebrities as soon as their books became available for purchase. Why?

The most interesting thing to me is that both deal with the supernatural, and neither woman considered herself to be much of a writer. Yet, both managed to create characters and stories that have sold millions of books, and their franchises have taken in millions from TV and/or movies.

How does that happen? In my opinion, it happens when the enemy of our souls gets behind it. This is not to say that either one of these women are *possessed.* It is also not to say that there is necessarily anything wrong with being successful. What is certainly strange though is *how* these women went from nobodies one day, to known celebrities the next, and all because of their created stories in which the supernatural plays a *huge* part.

Meyer, a Mormon homemaker, went from a normal life to superstar because of her one "vivid dream" she experienced, which was related to vampires. This happened literally overnight, in the space of six months. Rowling's story is even more interesting, going from living on welfare to authoring arguably one of the most sought after

[5] http://www.stepheniemeyer.com/twilight.html
[6] Ibid

characters in the 21st century, which made her a multi-millionaire in the space of five years, now worth nearly $800 million.[7]

These are *not* accidents. These are planned by forces, which are working to bring about their own purposes throughout the world. Have you ever wondered how a woman on welfare could write so many books? This is not to say that Rowling is an idiot, because there are many reasons that people go on welfare, and not all of them are about adopting a lifestyle of taking what you have not earned.

However, if you consider how *prolific* Rowling must be to write the number and *size* of books she has written about Harry Potter. This, in my mind, is *abnormal*, and requires help from beyond. Since Meyer attributes her book's story and characters to the dream she had, one would almost say the same thing about her, especially given her connections with what most believe to be a cult; Mormonism.

So what is going on here? It seems clear enough that Nephilim demons and fallen angels are working overtime to ensure that the world becomes desensitized to the supernatural. The goal is to make people think that the supernatural as seen in franchises like Harry

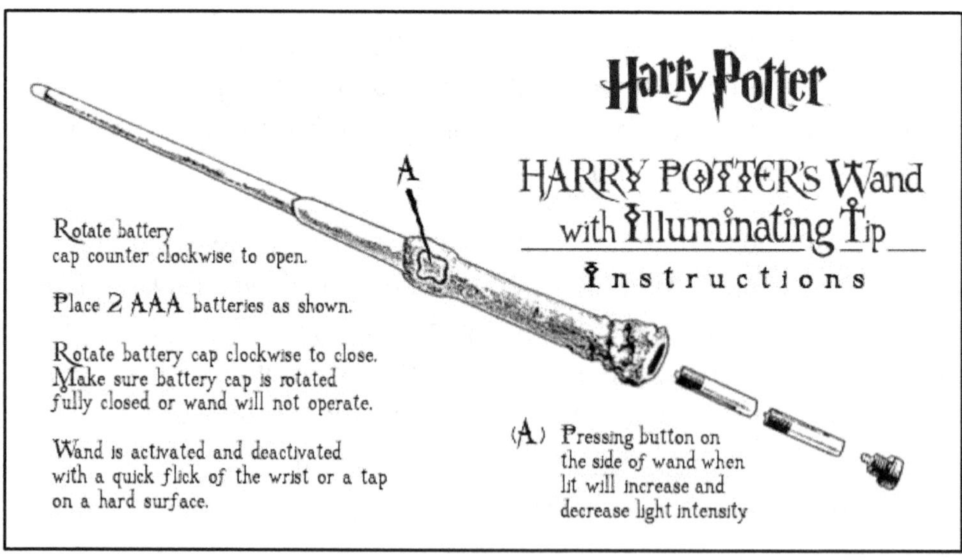

Potter and Twilight is perfectly normal and acceptable.

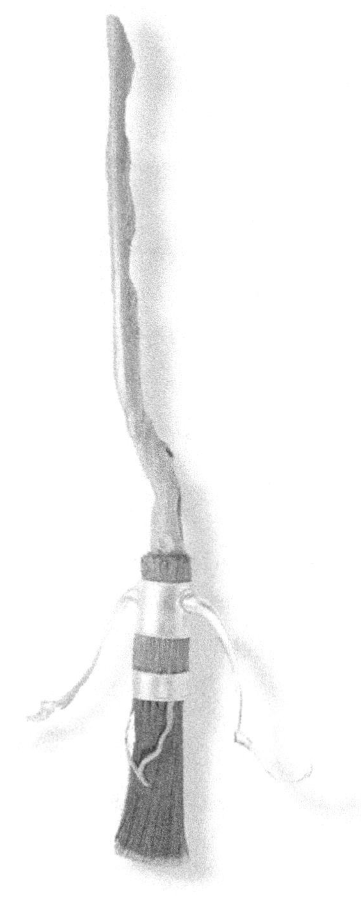

Would it be considered weird if kids could actually use the spells they hear about and see on the silver screen in real life? Not only would it *not* be considered weird, but also in reality, I almost think that kids are disappointed because they cannot at this time authentically do the things that Potter and his friends do in the movies.

The characters in the Potter films are in every respect, *ordinary* kids. They have their problems, their doubts, their frustrations and in short, they have loads of growing pains. Kids can and do relate to these characters. Who would not like to be able to cast a spell on the school bully so that he stops bothering you?

Who would not like to turn someone into a toad? Who would not like to be able to ride a real broom across the sky? Of course, movie franchises like these are not complete without companies who create licensed collectibles for kids (and adults) to spend money on so that they can recreate scenes from these movies.

Warner Bros., the Noble Collection, and other companies are producing a growing line of collectibles to suit everyone's needs. Some of the magic wands light up (as seen in the illustration on the previous page), to give a more realistic effect when casting a spell.

The fact that these movies are doing so well throughout the world says a great deal. *"As on Nov. 27, 2009, New Moon has taken in $338,174,000 Worldwide and it already holds the record for the #1 Yearly Opening Weekend in 2009, The #1 Opening Day Gross, The #1 Single Day Gross, the #1 Single Day Friday Gross, the #1 Opening Weekend in November, the #1 Opening Weekend on a Holiday, the #1 Widest Independent Releases, the #1 Widest Opening Independent Releases and the Fastest to $100 million!*[8]

It appears as though people cannot get enough of these types of movies, even buying up items like the one shown on the top of this page; a USB drive with 2GB of space for storage, complete with the vampire logo used in the movie.

There is something dangerously wrong when people clamor after these types of movie and artifacts as if they are the real thing. People seemingly are finding it more difficult to separate fact from fiction because the forces of darkness have increasingly sought to blend to two together into one. They have been blurring the line of demarcation until it will become virtually non-existent.

One of the things that has brought this about more than ever is the area of digital special effects. Years ago, effects were obvious. Not so today. It is at times difficult to tell when reality stops and digital

[8] http://www.twilightcollectors.com/

effects begin. This one area of filmmaking has set the stage for many of the illusions that may come into play with the coming Antichrist.

This was not the case years ago. Even *Dark Shadows*, a daytime soap, which also made it to the big screen, though scary, was clearly fantasy. However, everything that has come *before* Twilight and Harry Potter, were simply precursors and stepping-stones to bring us to where we are now.

Consider the fact that over the past decade, many of the movies that have been produced have ventured into the supernatural, and over time, the reality of the supernatural portrayed in these movies has been stepped up, until everything on the screen *seems* real and therefore very possible. This is due also to the advance of the aforementioned special effects industry. Because of increased technology, special effects can now be produced in *post-production*. Effects are created in programs like Adobe's After Effects, and they merge with the actual film without a glitch. Most people cannot tell the difference between when a person is acting out a scene, and where the acting stops and the special effects take over.

In the movie *Batman Begins*, a number of scenes were created completely by special effects. This becomes obvious in the scenes where actor Christian Bale is gracefully flying over Gotham City; however, special effects were also used during scenes where Bale's Batman would drop off a stairway onto the floor, encircled by thousands of bats.

While it might have been obvious to the viewer that the bats were created in post-production, what is probably *not* obvious is the fact that the entire scene was created in special effects, including Bale's Batman as he jumped from the stairway to the floor. The camera simply filmed the empty stage with the stairway, floor, and walls in place. Later, in post-production, all the other elements were added. Who knew? How would anyone be able to tell?

Since the late 1990s, the reality and creativity of many vampire and werewolf-related movies has been ramped up. The Blade triology, starring Wesley Snipes, where his character – a half-breed; human and vampire – goes on the hunt for other vampires to rid them from the face of the earth. This trilogy brought in millions.

Buffy, the Vampire Slayer started as a movie, and then went to the small screen as a TV series. With a bit of tongue-in-cheek, the main character, Buffy, learns that she must hunt down and destroy vampires. The movie, released in 1992, gave birth to the TV series, which aired from 1997 to 2003. Many of the characters in this series – as weird as they looked – were accepted as normal, even one particular character who looked like the devil incarnate, complete with horns. The character was affable, quirky, and very intelligent.

All of these movies, TV series, comic books, and graphic novels have made vampirism a household word. It has become normal to believe in the supernatural. None of this has been by accident. It has all been planned. However, lest we give Satan and his minions too much credit, it must be observed that all of this has transpired under God's watchful eye. All of these things have come to the fore because God, in His infinite wisdom, has allowed them to do so, because they direct the earth to His preordained plan.

The bottom line is that *because* of the increased interest in the supernatural vampire, lycanthrope, and Harry Potter trend, people are being programmed to accept this type of supernatural as *normal* and because of that, when they see someone who will actually do miracles, they will believe that this is also normal.

The Bible says that the Antichrist (man of sin) will come onto the scene and will eventually deceive because he is able to perform miraculous things and everyone will see them throughout the world and will marvel (cf. Revelation 13:3-7, 11-15).

Because the entire world is becoming obsessed with vampires, werewolves, and the supernatural, when the gates of hell are thrust open and the many demons and fallen angels are allowed their freedom for a time to roam, destroy, and torture using supernatural power, people will see these things and understand that what they have wished for has come true. Woe to them for it, as it will be much more than that for which they bargained.

Unfortunately, people see the strength of the vampires, and the power of Harry Potter, and that is what they want to have for *themselves*. Little do they realize that it is that kind of power that they will be on the *receiving* end of, from Nephilim demons and fallen angels who hate humanity because man was made in God's image.

Chapter 4

Smells Like Teen Spirit

More people are looking to the skies than ever before. More individuals are also reporting sightings of UFOs, or aliens or both. An increase in alien abduction of humans is also reportedly on the rise. Sightings of "Mothman," "The Grinning Man," and other supernatural phenomena are becoming normal.

Earthquakes and More

Something is obviously going on that has brought more of these events to the forefront. People are talking about these things as if they are part of the typical fabric of life on planet earth. Fewer and fewer people remain unconvinced that these things are untrue.

As I write this, our planet is obviously also experiencing enormous changes. Just a few weeks ago, a massive earthquake rocked Haiti to the point that little remains.

I went to one geological website, which reported that from February 20, 2010 to February 27, 2010, there were **213** earthquakes ranging from **2.2 to 8.8**, with most of them being in the 4.0 to 6.0 range.[9] It appears that a preponderance of earthquakes happened in the Chilean area. The Haitian earthquake that occurred a few weeks prior to the Chilean earthquake really had back-to-back earthquakes, the first measuring 4.6 followed by a 4.8, leaving ruins in its wake.

An earthquake measuring 8.8 on the Richter scale rolled through Chile just a few weeks ago. That earthquake was apparently so large that it shifted the earth off its axis, and wound up shortening the day by 1.26 microseconds. According to meteorologists, this occurred as the tectonic plates moved, compressing the areas of solid earth underneath and around it. Because of this compression, earth's rotational axis changed.

It is obvious that we will not notice the difference in time, but the fact remains that it happened. Also because of this earthquake, a number of tsunamis resulted, which further devastated the area of Chile.

On March 4, a 6.4 magnitude earthquake hit Taiwan, just days after the Chilean earthquake. This particular area is still in recovery from a typhoon that hit the area this past August 2009. The New York Times noted that there have been over 120 aftershocks in this area, some of which have measured 4.7 and 5.1. The last quake to hit this same area occurred in 1999, with 2400 deaths from a magnitude 7.6 quake.

One website, reporting on these earthquakes states, "*All of the earthquakes occurring lately are* ***starting to seem a bit alarming.***

---

[9] http://neic.usgs.gov/neis/qed/

Haiti, Chile, and now Taiwan have all experienced significant earthquakes in 2010. The United States is a bit overdue for an earthquake in the Western regions of the country according to some earthquake experts."[10]

What is the point? It is simply that the earth itself is going through massive *birth pangs*. You have undoubtedly heard that before and it has been true then, as it is true now. Just as a woman can be in labor for hours or days, when Christ spoke of the birth pangs of this planet (cf. Matthew 24), He did not indicate how long these birth pangs would last, but indicated that they would be the beginning of the end.

Anyone who can see should be able to understand that things are building to a crescendo. We have more alien phenomenon, people becoming more evil, and the planet itself feels like it is trying to toss people off, like a dog shaking itself after getting wet from a bath. We cannot underscore the fact enough that we are in the Last Days. They are upon us and if they are upon us, then it is obvious that everything else Christ foretold will happen as planned too. Though many may choose to deny it, there is no escaping it.

It would appear that this planet has a specific amount of time left, which of course, has also been determined by God. The fate of this planet and everything on it has always been His to determine.

Pleiadians Weigh In

However, the Pleiadians and other space aliens easily explain all of this away. They agree that the incidences of earthquakes is increasing (Richard Abanes was 100% wrong in more ways than one, in his book *End Times Delusion*, in which he stated that it only *appeared* as though earthquakes were on the rise – ed.). The Pleiadians explain that the main reason earthquakes are happening

---

10 http://www.associatedcontent.com/article/2759605/64_earthquake_hits_taiwan_march_2010.html

more and more, is due to the concentrated energy from *people. "It is this highly concentrated form of energy, which can make the Earth literally move."*[11]

Anyone who takes the time to observe it will recognize that people are becoming more brutal, less loving, less caring, and much more self-centered. It really does not take a genius to understand that this is the case. However, all of this can be easily ignored by those who wish to do so. These folks are interested in some *higher* power, gained from higher spiritual learning. Never mind that this higher learning is actually something that other-worldly beings teach is already resident in each human being. For those not interested in this higher level of alleged human *evolvement*, then the underbelly of society beckons. Those stuck in between these two groups do not know what to make of things, having neither foot in either camp.

What is also intriguing is the view of the afterlife held by all three different groups (and we are talking about people who remain unsaved here). To the New Age aficionado, they look for a progressively better world and life, in which their spiritual journey will take them to places of *euphoria*. There, they will become ascended masters themselves, enabled to reach back into this dimension to help those who need it and desire it.

To the person who is drawn more toward violence and committing acts of evil, they also will get what they want, or at least feel as though they will be getting what they want. Entities abound who are more than willing and able to infiltrate the lives of these individuals, creating within them the ability to be sordidly evil.

That's Right, We Bad

It seems that a preponderance of people within our society are preoccupied with coming across as "bad," or "mean." They like the

[11] Lia Shapiro *Comes the Awakening* (Star Street Press, 2000), 134

idea that people get the "don't mess with me" aura from them as they walk down the street, or drive their cars. What often provides fuel to these people are the images created by much of the hardcore music today.

I grew up listening to the basic Top-40 music. Remember "*Sugar, Sugar*" by the Archies? How about "*Dancin' in the Moonlight*" by King Harvest? Each decade had its own particular style of music. Even though everyone thought "rock 'n roll" was dead due to the invasion of disco, it came back in a major way not long after disco began to die and fade from the scene.

As rock music climbed once again to the top of the charts, this neew form of rock music was like nothing that which came before it. The days of the melodic rock bands like Journey, Boston, Kansas and others were quickly fading away, along with their many love songs.

Along with these groups were other hard rock groups like Led Zeppelin, Black Sabbath (with lead singer Ozzy Osbourne eventually going off on his own), as well as other well known groups like Deep Purple, The Scorpions, AC/DC and KISS.

While many of these groups continued throughout the 1970s and 80s, the late 1970s and early 80s gave birth to what became known as Punk Rock. Not only was this style of "music" something that deliberately pulled away from the mainstream, but it did so by creating music that was faster, more dissonant, and raucous. Beyond this, the individuals in these groups seemed to have no moral fiber whatsoever. Sid Vicious of the infamous Sex Pistols was so violent that he wound up stabbing his girlfriend to death; however, he was so drugged up at the time that he did not remember all the details. Eventually, Vicious accidentally overdosed on heroin.

Groups like Metallica, Judas Priest, Iron Maiden, and others also flourished at that time because of their onstage presence and the style of music. Normally, they played to full houses, with powerhouse guitar.

Anyone who knows any history of rock music knows that these groups had (and still have) large fan bases. Their fans eat up the music they produce. Much of the music is *depressing*, or feeds the resident anger within the fans.

In reality, Nephilim demons and fallen angels have been behind the music scene for decades. Depending upon the particular music group, fans heard the continual message of "*it's okay to sleep around*," or "*I'm so angry I'd like to hurt you*." While neither of these phrases were part of songs that existed (as far as this author knows), the messages were there in abundance.

Drugs, a huge part of the music scene was also prevalent at many to most rock concerts. At every turn, rock music was saturating young people with messages of rebellion, hatred, sex, and drugs. As long as the music had a decent beat to it and sounded good, to most kids, it really did not matter what they lyrics stated.

Rap Music Makes Us Badder Still

Today, Rap music seems to be on top. Other groups like Metallica still exist and make plenty of money, but Rap is where everything sits right now.

Starting in the hip hop generation of the various 'hoods in large cities, it was a way for African American youth, who felt disenfranchised from the mainstream, to grab their own reality and make their lives what they wanted them to be. In many cases, being signed as a Rap artist meant a way out of the ghetto, or 'hood.

The trouble of course, is that with Rap music (and frankly, I'm not sure why they call it music, since it is normally an angry person rhyming to a beat), let it all hang out. Most of the Rap music produced has filthy lyrics, and denigrating comments about women. It went from bad to worse.

The most remarkable thing about this type of music is when it is realized just how many *young white males* listen to it. In most ways these young men cannot at all relate to the lifestyle of the gangbanger living in East L.A., for instance, yet they claim it as their own.

From regular Rap, we got Gangsta Rap, which is exactly that; gangbangers or street gangsters putting their thoughts, ideas, and attitudes on a CD. Because of the type of verbiage used on many of these "songs," a number of wars have broken out, with one Rapper shooting another and the east coast rappers out to get the west coast rappers.

Violence certainly begets violence, and this style of music not only preaches it, but it winds up producing it as an offshoot. It is impossible to listen to this style of music without eventually getting angry.

Though a great many details have been left out of this brief historical retrospective, this has brought us to the point where we are now in today's society. People walk around with *attitude*, and a demeanor that essentially says that they are too tough for anyone to mess with, so we should avoid them.

In essence, the people who are *not* involved in some aspect of the New Age movement find solace (if that's the right word), in the outlooks created by today's music. Because of it, people have become far less inclined to care about their neighbors or their own actions. They have been taught through music throughout the preceding decades that if they do not look out for number one, who will.

I see it getting only worse as time progresses. I shudder to think of what might wind up being the in thing *after* Gangsta Rap has had its run. I recall my parents (along with many other parents of that day) being very upset when the Beatles hit our shores. Yet, compared to their first hits like "*I Wanna Hold Your Hand*," Gangsta Rap and other music of today is evil incarnate. It would actually be nice to get a bit of that innocence back, but it is too late for that. That time has come and gone.

Something New

Speaking of the Beatles, not only did they introduce a brand new style of music to the impressionable minds of young people everywhere, but Satan had designed it so that once they made it to the top, their weirdness began to kick in. From *Sgt Pepper's Lonely Heart's Club Band* to introducing Transcendental Meditation to America, these four young men from Liverpool, England literally changed the world. Of course, they did not change it without the persistent power of the forces of darkness behind them.

From there, people who were not necessarily interested in only what music had to offer began embracing what Transcendental Meditation offered. Essentially, this was the start of the New Age movement in America. Unfortunately, not only have we been unable to go back to the innocence prior to that time, but also this movement has made tremendous gains into just about every area of society, including the visible Church.

Though some people vociferously disagree that New Age thought *has* infiltrated the church, it is clear that this is the case. One individual disagrees so strongly with the belief that the New Age has gained access inside the church has published a book about it. I wish I did not have to provide his name or the title of his book, because I hate giving him any kind of free publicity, but what can you do?

He has a free preview for his downloadable book and as an interested party, I took advantage of the opportunity to download it.

My comments here are then based only on that part of his book, which turns out to be the 15-page introduction alone.

The author of this book – Bill Slabaugh – wastes no time in getting to his point! I took the opportunity to download the free preview of his *The New Pharisaism* book, to determine whether I wanted to pay $12.95 to download the full eBook. At any rate, he begins by referring back to his school days when he remembered being bullied by the bigger kid in school. He managed to bypass the bully one day, only to meet him the next day whereupon this bully *bullied* him for not meeting him after school the previous day.

Workplace Bullies
From there, Slabaugh goes into a discussion of workplace bullying, which has happened to all of us. He then moves into a dialogue about bullying that often goes on in churches. Up to this point, there is nothing in his book with which I would disagree.

Slabaugh then moves onto the subject of what he refers to as the "new Pharisaism." Not the first one to use the phrase, he immediately segues into the alleged "tactics" of these modern Pharisees. He seems to hold nothing back when he states, "*For several years now, several national organizations have turned their sights on the church. As if we don't have enough false religions systems and cults to deal with, we are now **being attacked and threatened within** by those who call themselves Bible-believing Christians. This **contentious attack** has come by the way of books, newsletters, letters, emails, the internet, and blogs. This **inflammatory material** has made its way into the church through **individuals and small groups of bullies** who have used it **for their own selfish gain and self-styled agenda**. The weapons of their warfare consist of **destructive written material which has no true scriptural basis**. They are **self-appointed Pharisees** who refer to themselves as 'watchmen,' 'apprising ministries,' 'guardians of truth,' and 'discerning ministries.' **As a result of their intimidation and lies**, people are getting hurt,* *churches are being split, pastors are leaving the ministry and many churches and ministries have been rendered ineffective in the world, or closed-down altogether."*[12] (emphasis added) (You know, after reading the above comments, I'm beginning to think that Slabaugh never got over being bullied when he was a kid...)

Batter UP!

From this point, Slabaugh seems to just be getting warmed up. He's taken a few warm-up swings, and is now ready to knock the ball out of the park. First, aside from his name-calling, his definition of a Pharisee appears to be lacking. Beyond this, he also seems to be mixing up a few things here. Yes, there *are* bullies in churches. However, I have *yet* to run across a church bully who has the truth of the gospel as the reason for their alleged "bullying." They are normally bullies because of their own *wants.* Second, most bullies I have come across in church have absolutely *no* interest in spiritual things at all. In fact, his examples of church bullies (he refers to them as spiritual bullies) prove this. He refers to the church secretary who spreads damaging gossip about the pastor or someone else in the church, or the choir director who insists he will quit if he doesn't get his way, then there's the pastor who bullies his way through board meetings or refuses to allow people in the congregation to have their way. I would have to agree that these people *do* in fact, exist in nearly all church settings that I have been associated with, or heard about. This is not uncommon, or new. Yet, Slabaugh has no problem making this huge jump from these individuals (who may not even be authentic Christians, but merely those who *profess* to having salvation), to linking them with people like Jan Markell from Olive Tree Ministries, or other folks (and he names them).

Bill is Right – All Who Disagree with Him are Wrong

The other problem I have with Slabaugh's commentary is that he makes *declarative* statements, completely *lacking in love.* He

---

[12] Bill Slabaugh *The New Pharisaism* (2010), 12

dogmatically declares that what people like Jan Markell do is *without biblical support.* I have a problem with that, not only because I believe him to be seriously wrong, but also because while we are all tempted to make these statements, it really is incumbent upon us to present these views as our opinion *with* biblical support. We do this, understanding that there may be the potential to be wrong.

Slabaugh claims that the new Pharisee – the spiritual bully – gets his or her way in the church, by lording it over others to intimidate them, and spiritually abuse them. Yeah, I have to say that Jan Markell is truly a force to reckon with. Whew, I start shaking every time I see even a photo of her! What a *meanie* she is! That is the power that Markell has and wields! She is THE most intimidating person I have ever seen! Lord, protect me, please!

Slabaugh also claims that these new Pharisees major in minor doctrinal points and they supposedly redefine biblical terms. Frankly, I'm not sure what is so minor about *salvation,* which is the main sticking point, but maybe to him, salvation is minor, I don't know. To me, it is *major,* not minor. Maybe Bill just wants people to be happy, and doggone it, if they are happy traveling a labyrinth, which covers the floor of a sanctuary during a spiritual growth exercise, well then who cares if that labyrinth is based on the same one the Druids used. So what if people want to use "breath prayers" in which the mind is set in neutral, while the Alpha wave patterns take over. C'mon, we just need to all lighten up a bit, don't we?

Who is Revising What?

I have lost track of how many people accuse other people of either historical or biblical *revisionism.* That along with calling someone a *heretic* are very easy claims to make. When he also states that the arguments are mainly over minor doctrinal points, it seems clear that he has no clue, but obviously believes himself to be in the "major" doctrinal area.

What I see from Olive Tree Ministries, Understanding the Times and other ministries is a desire to keep the gospel *pure* from error. That was *not* the intent of the Pharisees. They intended only to keep themselves in their cherished position of religious *leader* and *hallowed cleric.* In today's day and age, I do not see the previously mentioned ministries as being in the *majority* at all. In fact, it is patently clear from the tone of the visible church that *most* people *clearly reject* the attempts by these ministries and others like them to warn people of impending disaster in the church. Slabaugh wants to paint an entirely different picture, of people lying broken on the street, having been ejected from this church or that one, and all because of people who want to keep the gospel *pure.* Now granted, I am very aware of how bullies in the church work. They are certainly *not* spiritual bullies by any stretch. They are *carnal* all the way around. The *last* thing they are worried about is any sort of mysticism gaining a foothold in the church. In fact, if it suits their purpose, they will proclaim it from one end of the sanctuary to the other!

The Pharisees of Christ's day were *never* questioned by anyone. Their word was *law.* They were honored in the streets and people would actually *bow* as these men walked by. As Christ claimed, the Pharisees made it nearly impossible for people to gain salvation because it was buried under layers and layers of rabbinical tradition. The Pharisees in general did not have salvation either. So, maybe Slabaugh is *implying* that the people he is referring to as the New Pharisees do not have authentic salvation either, who knows. He came extremely close to saying it, without saying it in his introduction.

I'm Not Seeing It

I'm simply not seeing the connection at all between the Pharisees of Jesus' day and the alleged Pharisee of today that Slabaugh's speaks of, at least in the form of the ministries and people he *labels*

Pharisees. While I *do* agree that the church has always had its share of Pharisees, Slabaugh's definition of a Pharisee is way off. Did he learn that at Dallas Theological Seminary? If you were asked to say one word that defined the Pharisee of Christ's day, you would probably say *legalistic*, or something similar.

The alleged Pharisees of today – at least the ones Slabaugh *says* are Pharisees – are not legalistic as the Pharisees of Christ's day were legalistic. A good example of the legalism of the Pharisees is when their parents needed help, but the Pharisees would respond, "*Oh darn, Mom, I WISH I could help, but I have already promised my extra money for this month to the Temple*" (cf. Matthew 15:1-20). This "corban" was merely an excuse the Pharisees used so they could get away with *not* helping their parents. Christ condemned it.

Another example of the legalism of the Pharisees is when they would promise to do something for someone and swear by the altar (You know, "*I swear by the altar that I will...*"). When it came to collect on the promise, the same Pharisee would say, "*Oh, you know what? I swore by the altar itself, instead of by the horns of the altar! I am excused from having to keep my promise to you.*" None of this is in evidence with the ministries he points to as being *Pharisaical.*

Slabaugh Seems to Be Missing His Own Point

The reality is that legalism and Pharisaism go hand in hand. I simply do not see that as Slabaugh has defined both the Pharisee of Jesus' day and the ones in ours. I *do* know people whom I would call Pharisees today and they are *exactly* like the Pharisees of Jesus' day; legalistic to a fault, hard-hearted, they are always right, and always find a way to turn things around so that they are exempt from any fault. They are backbiters, proud, disobedient; they reject authority and all the rest.

Slabaugh's big problem is that he believes these modern-day Pharisees apparently harp on what they see as "evils" that have penetrated the church, though he obviously sees these things as altruistic, and creating a tone of love in the church, or at least encouraging it. Things like Eastern Mysticism, aspects of the Occult, and other New Age practices, *have* gained access into the visible church (whether Slabaugh believes it or not), which began decades ago. Apparently, Slabaugh does not see this as having taken place in the church. He does not see the presence of mysticism, because to him, it is not there, so there is no problem! This makes me wonder what he calls all the mystical practices that actually *have* found their way into the church. I would assume that he embraces them, and does not like the fact that there are people who are calling what he embraces, *error.*

Sticks and Stones

He is so busy accusing, labeling, and name-calling that one wonders how he manages to think that he loves anyone with whom he disagrees, though he states that a loving approach should be used when running up against the modern Pharisee. Apparently, the new Pharisee comes across as *"very cult-like and is nothing less than an attack against the Church of Jesus Christ."*[13]

Um...okay, we *get* it, Bill. You do *not* like what the New Pharisee stands for. Here is what ***I*** do not like. I do not like the fact that Dallas Theological Seminary has gone so far off its moorings and graduates people like Bill Slabaugh who are obviously blind to the problems that *do* exist in the visible church.

While Paul says that we wrestle *not* against flesh and blood, here is yet one more person who clearly thinks we *do*. The problems in the church *exist* because of the many aspects of mysticism that have gained entry. This is a *spiritual problem,* foisted upon the visible Church through spiritual entities. In many cases, these areas of

[13] Bill Slabaugh *The New Pharisaism* (2010), 12

mysticism have gained total control of the way that church *worships*, and what the people in that congregation *believe*.

It's the Experience

Slabaugh not only does *not* agree with that, but my guess is that he sees the many forms of mysticism as creating a deep sense of *love* (emotion/experience). Because of the mysticism that has gained access to our congregations, many churches have become "super-sized." It is not uncommon to see or hear of a church with over 3, 4, 5, or 10 thousand people. In fact, there is one of these churches not far from where I live (that we *used* to attend), that boasts over 4,500 people. When you go there, it is a carnival atmosphere. They have a coffee shop on their "campus," there is food before and after each church service and a million things going on. People are excited! The music is LOUD, raucous, and even what I would call (as a drummer), *rock music*. These concerts (they call them worship services), are just that – *concerts*, that glorify the musicians and singers, not God.

The preaching at many of these churches is *nothing*. Some of the sermon titles are "*How to Gain More Friends*," or "*What To Do When You Don't Get That Job You Want*," or "*Grab the Gusto!*" or numerous other titles. Lest people think that these titles are merely titles to get people in the door, and then actual exposition starts from the pulpit, think again. A church service, which lasts for an hour to an hour and fifteen minutes usually, leaves no more than 20 minutes for a "sermon." The sermon is usually peppered with humor and quips throughout. The sermons are usually topical, which is one of the easiest ways to accidentally wind up teach error, since things are often taken out of their context. Nothing beats *verse-by-verse exposition*, and fewer and fewer pastors even know what that means, much less preach that way today.

Accusation After Accusation

Slabaugh's book is filled with rank *accusations*. In spite of the fact that he believes that all people (including the New Pharisees) should be handled with love, he is quick to point out that "*Pharisees resist godliness with all their self-righteous might.* ***Their religion*** *majors in the externals rather than the internal condition of the soul and the deepening of the person's love and intimacy with the Savior. They trust in themselves rather than trusting in God and they view others with contempt (Luke 18:9). They resist the very things they need to live a godly life.*"[14] (emphasis added) Slabaugh clearly seems to be stating that people like Jan Markell are *not* saved, which means he has entered into the area of *judging* people. The more he states, the less he seems to know.

Statements like the above are quite condemnatory, but the reason Slabaugh believes it is *okay* is that he has classified people as *Pharisees*, whether they are that or not. It does not really matter, because he has determined that this is what they are, so it must be true. If they are classified as Pharisees, then it is perfectly fine to *condemn* them. Isn't that what Jesus did?

Again, everything I have mentioned and quoted is from Slabaugh's 15-page introduction (free preview). I am afraid to read the rest of it, for fear of the pages bursting into flames by the time I get to the end of the book. I am sure there will be more name-calling, labeling, castigation, and condemnation, yet supposedly asserted *in love.*

My opinion is that Slabaugh is *confused.* He is confused about the Pharisees of Jesus' day and he is confused about those who appear to be fighting to keep the gospel *pure.* It also appears that while Slabaugh is interested in *love,* he seems to define it as an intimacy with the Savior, which then relegates it to the area of *feeling*, and feeling does not have to be based on *truth.* It simply has to feel *good.* It is based on *feeling*, which stems from an individual's *experience.* While there is nothing wrong with feelings, I have to wonder why he believes he can make the types of statements he

[14] Bill Slabaugh *The New Pharisaism* (2010), 15

makes and fear no retributive action from the very Lord he says he worships, *if* he is wrong.

Jesus and Paul

If Jesus decided to go head to head with the Pharisees, that was His business. If Paul, as a chosen apostle of the Lord believed he had the authority (and he did), to take on the "Judaizers" of Galatians, even wishing that they would all the way and emasculate themselves because of the issue of circumcision, that was Paul's decision. Slabaugh would likely argue that the people associated with the ministries he refers to as being Pharisaical, are calling out people like Rick Warren, Joel Osteen, and a ton of other people, who it certainly seems, Slabaugh *supports.*

The trouble though is that by all accounts, many individuals like Warren, Richard Foster, Osteen, etc., *do* seem to be introducing elements of mysticism into the church setting. The emphasis in many of these churches appears to be on *feeling* and *experience,* instead of on the *truth of Scripture.* Osteen's *Your Best Life Now* is a case in absurdity, yet the average churchgoer seems to gobble it up. They want their ears scratched and Osteen, among others certainly seems to measure up to the task.

Just as Slabaugh believes that what he is doing by writing his book is something that glorifies the Lord, the people he *condemns* would say that they believe what they are doing is something that glorifies the Lord as well. The reality is that both cannot be correct, and both (including Slabaugh) must come under the truth of Scripture. Ultimately, both *do* and *will.*

Who is Really a Pharisee?

It is funny (or maybe, ironic). When I read people like Jan Markell, Deborah Dumbrowski, Roger Oakland, or any number of these people, I *never* get the sense that they HATE the people they write about. It appears that what they say, they say with a near broken heart. On the contrary, when I read Slabaugh's 15-page introduction, I get a deep sense of anger and resentment from him. I could be wrong. However, because of the amount of vitriol in his opening comments, it appears that his underlying demeanor stems not from love, but from a near-hatred of those who are warning against what they see as *departure from the faith*.

It seems relatively clear that Slabaugh is angry about something and someone. I cannot help but wonder though if his anger is *misplaced*. He seems to be blending *two* different groups into one, which ultimately creates a group he labels *New Pharisaism*. Let's face it, who does *not* love to hate the Pharisees? It is my opinion that Slabaugh needs to back down just a trifle, and take the time to determine whether there is any truth in what the people he calls Pharisees are saying. Certainly, he is convinced that his opinion is the correct one. I am assuming he would go on to say that, there is *no* Emergent Church, *no* mysticism within the church, *no* eastern meditation, and certainly not that, which would be classified as New Age. It must all be a mirage then.

Unfortunately, all of my research has convinced me of the exact *opposite*. We have personally left two churches because of their slide into mysticism. (Slabaugh would likely be proud that we did not leave people broken and hurting on the curb as we left, I am sure.) The visible Church seems to have been infiltrated by New Age thought and mysticism. It has replaced the authority of God's Word with the alleged *authority of feelings and experience*. After all, if people *feel* more loving, then it must be true, right? Reminds me of the song, "If lovin' you is wrong, I don't want to be right."

Is Christianity Based on Truth or Feeling?

The truth of the matter is that Christianity is *not* based on *feelings*, or *experience*. It is based on truth and when that truth is shoved to the side, in favor of feelings, no matter how altruistic those feelings and experiences appear to be, something is drastically wrong.

Slabaugh, rather than being willing to direct his gaze at the visible Church to see if in fact, it *has* been overrun by mysticism, seems much more willing to do exactly what he says Christians *cannot* do; deal with the bullying Pharisee as Ralphie dealt with Scut Farkas in "A Christmas Story."

I cannot imagine what the rest of Slabaugh's book is like, and for a $12.95 price tag (for a downloadable eBook), I am hesitant to spring for it. The final irony though is that while he is accusing any number of ministries of self-glorification, profit, and self-aggrandizement by taking people's money for the books and DVDs they produce, I believe he himself is charging an excessive amount for his book. It is difficult to figure out why he thinks his book is worth $13.00 for something that I would have to print out on my own paper, with my own ink. Oh well, no one ever said critics were able to see their own flaws.

As of this writing, I had emailed him asking him how many pages his book was and why he is charging $12.95 for a downloadable eBook. No response yet, but I will certainly put his response on my BLOG[15] if I ever get one.

[15] www.studygrowknowblog.com

Chapter 5
All You Need is Love

Sweet love. If there is one thing people are looking for, yearning for, and desiring with all their hearts is to be loved. No one likes to be *unloved*. It does not feel good for one thing, and it creates a deep sense of hopelessness born of loneliness on the other.

God our Creator created us with the *capacity* to love others and to *receive* love ourselves. The fact that Adam and Eve essentially spurned that love by rejecting the truth of God put them on a continuing downward spiral of trying to replace God's love with something else entirely. Nothing can replace God's love in us because only He can fill the large hole in our hearts.

Unfortunately, those involved in the New Age movement believe that the love they seek are found within the teachings of their own movement. Because of this, more and more people are finding this movement attractive.

The Changing Face of the New Age

The New Age movement is unique in that it is always in style because of its ability to incorporate many forms. For those outside the visible and invisible Church, it promises to teach people about love totally apart from God. For those within the visible Church, by adding some Christian-sounding terminology, it becomes perfectly acceptable and *feels* right to many professing Christians.

Let's discuss those outside the church first though, because it is here that we come to realize the full potential of the movement, in all its various forms. The longer an individual stays in the movement, the more they come to realize that it all leads to the subject of *aliens*, who are visitors from other galaxies, come here to help us.

Scientology has for the longest time espoused the idea that the highest form of knowledge comes directly from aliens. I remember reading an interview/article about Tom Cruise and his stint in Scientology. When he learned that at the top of the ladder were *aliens* as ascended masters, he thought it was the most ridiculous thing he had ever heard (my paraphrase). Eventually, he came to understand and believe that it *must* be true, because there was simply too much alleged evidence to disregard it.

In a previous book I published called, *Demons in Disguise*, I spoke briefly about the group of aliens known as Pleiadians. The purpose of that book was not to delve too deeply into who they are and what they purpose to achieve. The purpose of this book *will* include that and in my research, I have come across some invaluable information that sheds the light on this area.

We are going to begin with a woman named Lia Shapiro. The title of one of her books that we will be referring to is *Comes the Awakening,* which has the subtitle *Realizing the Divine Nature of Who You Are.* The back dust jacket is filled with a number of positive reviews from five people who rave about Lia's book. One person – Ronna Herman – claims that she channels the *Archangel Michael.* Another individual claims to channel other Pleiadians.

According to these folks, people like Michael, the Archangel, as well as the plethora of alien hosts, strongly desire to bring us peace and love. They wish to break our negative chains from what controls us in order that we would be free indeed.

As we open her book, Lia intones the word, *"I offer thanks to the Spirit within, the Pleiadians who exist as a part of me, and Spirit/God beyond which is a part of us all and connects us."*[16]

Chapter One opens the door to Lia's earlier years to us, before she realized that she was a Pleiadian herself. For Lia, time is not important. What is important is *knowledge* leading to *love,* or was it love leading to knowledge?

She readily admits that she was a hippie, filled with protesting, love beads, bellbottom jeans and all the rest, including the VW *"painted in a dazzling profusion of colors."*[17] It was also a time in her life of spiritual awakening for her and many others like her.

For someone like me who never experienced the drug culture or the hippie movement (except as an outside observer), it is difficult for me to put myself in that situation emotionally. Yet, at the same time, it was clearly an experience, which freed Lia from conventional thought and wisdom. That makes sense.

---

[16] Lia Shapiro *Comes the Awakening* (Star Street Press, 2000), 5

[17] Ibid, 10

The one thing she makes clear is that aside from all that the hippie movement came to be known for, it was "*the* energy *of those times that stirred [her] soul and started an awakening deep within [her].*"[18] She readily admits to no formal religious training of any type, and essentially found her own path, she believes on her own.

The one thing that pops up repeatedly (and it does not matter if it is with Lia Shapiro, or anyone else from various aspects of the New Age movement), the belief that truth is found *within* each individual is tantamount. It is truly the most important part of all that they seek. Searching diligently *within* is the key that unlocks the hidden realities associated with our latent "deity."

The more time Lia spent deep within herself, the more beautiful her experiences became she claims. She laments at how difficult it is for mere words to describe experiences of that magnitude. What is also interesting of course is how individuals like Sharpiro, though admitting to have no formal training in any particular area of religion, quickly become *theologians* themselves because of these experiences.

So THAT'S How It Happened!

She states that during one of her inner experiences, she came face to face with Jesus Himself. This experience was a moment of true spiritual bliss. Her impression of Jesus is important to note, in her own words. *"He did not speak but I heard him say, 'See, this is where we go.' He was not the Jesus that the Bible has made of him, but he was as we are. He had simply brought truths from a higher realm...and they turned him into the Son of God."*[19] The fact that she *knew* the individual was Jesus, yet it was not the Jesus from the Bible is interesting to note. How did she know that? Obviously, the many pieces of art associated with Him would have come into play here.

---

[18] Lia Shapiro *Comes the Awakening* (Star Street Press, 2000), 11
[19] Ibid, 12

From here, Shapiro determined that we are all "Suns" and we actually come from the "Light." She says she experienced this Light and all at once, forces overcame her that are difficult to explain, yet can only best be explained through the pictures that adjectives create. She felt filled with *joy*, overpowered by *love*, which indwelt and filled her from top to bottom.

Shapiro also indicates that it was at this point that she traveled the many layers of the universe and as she did so, the eternal knowledge of that universe came to her, systematically. Her revelation led her to understand that this is where God existed, "*not outside of me, but inside and at the very highest level of my being! Inside every creation in the universe, God is dwelling there. You are God. I am God. We are all God and God is us!*"[20]

Of course, those of us who have been studying anything to do with the New Age movement (truly a religion of its own making), understand that this has always been the message. The only thing that really changes is *how* that message is delivered and by whom it is delivered through.

For Shapiro, this experience brought sweeping changes in her life because she had "*gone through a major, spiritual, evolutionary leap.*"[21] Her in-laws, who happened to be staunch fundamentalist Baptists, believed that Lia's experience was an actual *conversion to Christianity*, so they immediately began instructing her in the basics of the Bible. She got completely caught up into this and began studying the Bible for herself, and determined to follow the Bible *only*.

Circumstances eventually led her out of the country, first to Africa, then to Japan. It was here, while still believing that she was a Christian, she encountered Japanese *spirituality*. One woman

---

[20] Lia Shapiro *Comes the Awakening* (Star Street Press, 2000), 13

[21] Ibid, 15

referred to Shapiro as "light," and told her "*You will have a mission in the world.*"[22]

It was through that individual – named Shigeko – that she learned of *UFOs* and *pyramids*, as well as other things that piqued her interest and imagination. Shapiro began to have powerful dreams and visions, some of which felt so strong, that she came to believe they had been actual *encounters*.

Close Encounters Redux

Right out of a scene from *Close Encounters of the Third Kind*, she began drawing triangles, just as some of the characters in that movie had become preoccupied with the image of the Devil's Tower (aka Devil's Postpile), in Wyoming, and were constantly recreating it through drawings and sculptures. From here, while she says she has always been a writer, she found herself at her computer writing what came into her head. When she read it, it was as if someone else had written it, so new were the thoughts that had been written in sentences on her paper.

Shapiro believes that one day she stopped being a Christian altogether. It is clear from her own testimony and the truth of Scripture that she had *never been a Christian*, but was merely *told* that she had a conversion to Christianity. When she says she stopped being a Christian altogether, what actually happened was that she stopped practicing externally the things that Christians do, like praying, reading the Bible, etc. There had been no spiritual rebirth that I can discern from her own words.

After experiencing numerous highs and lows, and a near fatal bout with meningitis, she discovered that her purpose on earth was to bring to the world the wisdom of the *Pleiadians*. While they are *not* God, they exist in a higher realm or plane, with God being overall.

[22] Ibid, 18

She states that her understanding of time is such that it is not *linear*. From this revelation, she understands that she exists in the *present*, the *past*, and the *future* all at once. Though human in this present period, she attests that she is Pleiadian in the future. Her desire is that we find out who we are in our future, for it may be that we are also Pleiadian as well.

Chapter Two of Shapiro's book goes into a religious history of the world, starting with the time *prior* to man's arrival on planet earth. Instead of Jesus Christ being the actual Alpha and Omega, humanity holds that title apparently. Shapiro is just getting warmed up though because the end of chapter two states, "*Know that, however, this book came to be in your hands, it is indeed for* you. *There is a message contained in these pages and it would behoove you to continue reading. It is for you to find out the truth of yourself that is hidden beneath the layers, locked away deeply. If you listen carefully,* **we** *will help to unlock the secrets.*"[23] (emphasis added)

You will notice the reference to "we" in Shapiro's last sentence quoted above. She includes herself in the Pleiadian collective and they offer the vast wealth of knowledge as a gift to humanity. Where have we heard this before, and *why* are all these messages about *religion*, without fail? Interestingly enough, the average New Ager never seems to tire of hearing these sermons by our spaced-out invaders to this planet. In spite of the fact that it is the same ol' rigmarole stated slightly differently, the core message is always the same.

As we continue through Shapiro's book, we will also be focusing on two other books, which purport to provide greater insight into the Pleiadian agenda. Do they ever really say what it is they want and why they are here, other than all the religious instruction and terminology they utilize? We shall see...

---

[23] Lia Shapiro *Comes the Awakening* (Star Street Press, 2000), 25

Chapter 6

Stairway to Heaven

What I always find fascinating whenever I read through another book written by someone who channels some great being from *beyond* the great beyond, is the constant mix of biblical truths with replacement facts. What I mean by that is that while these Nephilim demons are busy impersonating benevolent space truckin' beings, they take biblical truth and *modify* it so that while the core of the truth, story, or parable continues to be present, many of the smaller details are changed so that they take on new meaning.

However, since the core of the story remains the same, this fact may be either completely overlooked by the average individual, or not questioned if these changes are noticed, simply because so many people tend to view areas of Scripture allegorically anyway. This is of course, nothing new at all, since the Reformed, Covenant, and Preterist approach to prophetic Scripture has always been to view things allegorically. Unfortunately, as I am sure you are aware, this approach leaves little room for objectively understanding those parts of Scripture since the individual determines meaning *subjectively*.

That is at least one reason we have so many different interpretations out of there related to the End Times. There is little consistency because many people take various parts of Scripture to mean something yet are unable to adequately show how they arrive at that position.

The same is true with Shapiro's book here. Though these are not stating to be her revelations, they *are* implied to be the revelations from the Pleiadians. Because of that, the question, which rises to the surface from the New Age perspective is, "*why would the Pleiadians lie to us?*"

Why No One Questions Them

Actually, a far more important question is whether the so-called Pleiadians have done anything at all to prove their own identity. The answer to that question is a resounding and unqualified *no*. However, you see what has happened here. The Pleiadians come from "out there somewhere." Because they *seem* to possess an intrinsic and almost god-like knowledge of all things within our universe, their identity would of course, *not* be doubted at all.

If their identity is never doubted, then why would anyone doubt the veracity of their message(s)? You see, the Nephilim demons and fallen angels have successfully pulled the wool over the eyes of multitudes. They have actually done what is difficult to do, by getting human beings to believe that they are whom they say they are – *Pleiadians.* Because people believe *that* with little to no difficulty, believing what these beings tell them is accepted eagerly. It really goes hand in hand.

Numerous televangelists use this same trick. They are often very magnetic and their message is compelling. Because they tend to speak with an air of authority, they are normally not questioned. When they are questioned, the individual doing the questioning is made to look like a lamebrain, numbskull, or modern-day Pharisee.

Don't Worry...Be Wealthy!

I remember years ago, there were people (and still are), who touted the ways a person could become nearly instantly wealthy. In essence, it was done by subterfuge, sleight of hand and outright lying. I remember reading parts of one book and the one statement that stuck out in my mind was that if people want to *be* wealthy, they must *act* as if they *are* wealthy. It sounds simplistic and almost too easy. However, this is exactly what the proverbial *con man* does.

There were easy ways to accomplish this stated the author of the book I was perusing. First, go out and get fake business cards made up. Spend a bit of money on them to make them look nice, something that would impress the average individual. This was before cell phones, so it was even suggested that you hire an answering service (not a machine, but a live service) to take your phone calls. Since only businesses did that at the time, it would be automatically assumed that you were a business. If anyone called to check up on you, there would be a real person to answer the phone and take your messages for you. You would be able to call at any time and receive your messages.

Another way to look wealthy was by renting an expensive car and driving it to events where the press would be. This might even include crashing a party (but of course, acting as if you belonged there and becoming extremely indignant when you discover that your name was left off the guest list). This incident might even wind up in the society page of the local paper.

The whole point of all this was to *look*, or come across as already being wealthy. This would work in your favor because soon, other (real) wealthy people would take notice of you, and begin to bring you in to their inner circle. As I continued to read the book, I had to laugh because depending upon how you looked at it, the author was telling you to become a con artist, or an actor. In either case though, you would be presenting a lie to people and depending upon how good of an actor you were, they would either believe it or not. We have all seen movies in which professional con artists are able to circumvent the authorities all because they know people very well, *and* they are excellent actors. That is the most important part of any con, from all that I have read.

Your Mission...

The TV show *Mission Impossible*, based every scenario on this belief. It was a great show that kept you on the edge of your seat because there was always the inevitable potential of being caught. No one ever was, and *if* that could have happened, there was always *Plan B*.

One of my favorite episodes guest-starred William Shatner. His character - Thomas Kroll – was one of the murderers that had killed someone in 1937. The IMF team literally took him back in time. They recreated his old neighborhood, temporarily got rid of the limp he had developed over the years, and made him believe that he was still living in that period. It was fascinating the way they made it happen.

Of course, by the end of the hour, just minutes prior to the end of that episode, Shatner's character's life began to unravel before him. His limp came back, things started to fall apart, and by the time he fully realized what happened, he had already given IMF the secrets they needed to know; the location of the body of the person he had helped kill.[24]

All of this espionage works because of the quality of the *acting*. The more believable the presentation, the more believable the message. This is what Nephilim demons and fallen angels *know* about humanity. We are gullible and because we do not have all the facts, we can be conned. The Bible only gives slight glimpses behind the curtain into the spiritual realm. We do not have all the facts. It is so easy to see, just in the first few chapters of Shapiro's book. She believes that she actually travelled the layers of the universe, and saw and experienced marvelous sights! Yet, we see little to nothing of what the Bible tells us actually exists in our universe, and we will get to that shortly.

If you travel back to the music of the 1960s and 70s, aside from what has already been discussed, it is easy to find songs that have a decided *ethereal* quality to them. This is not necessarily referring to the music itself, although that certainly existed in the 1970s and later. Rock bands like Led Zeppelin hit the charts with songs that made us go, "Hmmm, I wonder what they are *really* saying". Their tune *Stairway to Heaven*, was a staple once it released to the world via a live performance in 1971. By 1973, the song had grown in popularity throughout the world and was understood to be other-worldy. In fact, Robert Plant, the band's lead vocalist and lyricist, credits what he had been reading at the time. The books written by James Lewis Thomas Chalmbers Spence, were highly occultic due to Spence's own interests and ideology.[25]

Songs like *Stairway* and others were an outgrowth of the early movement prior to the New Age movement, which essentially grew out of the hippie movement. Even the rock group Three Dog Night

---

[24] http://www.imdb.com/title/tt0649230/
[25] http://en.wikipedia.org/wiki/Stairway_to_Heaven

had its share of peculiar hits, like "*Shambala*." The word "Shambala" refers to the hidden, mythical kingdom by the same name from Tibetan literature. It relies heavily on eastern mysticism. Who would have thought? I liked it because it had a beat and you could dance to it.

The Bible *never* attempts to prove the existence of the One, True God of the universe. The Bible simply *assumes* His existence. Shapiro's book simply does what the Bible does in this regard. This is what the Pleiadians and every other space alien group does, taking their cue from Scripture. They do not spend time trying to prove their existence and that they are who or what they say they are, but they simply present themselves as if we would be morons *not* to accept their existence as they are presented. The very fact that they are talking with human beings *proves* they exist. However, it does not prove that they are Pleiadians. That is taken for granted.

The major difference of course, between the Bible and the Pleiadians is the way in which people view them. For most, the Bible is an old, out of date, antiquated book written by a bunch of men. It is allegedly filled with all types of contradictions and because of those alleged contradictions, it cannot be trusted, nor is it trustworthy. By the same token, the God of the Bible is viewed much the same as the Bible that He wrote. He has not proven His existence to most, at least to their satisfaction (as if THE God of the universe must ask "How high?" when a human being says, "Jump!").

Yet while no such courtesy extends to the God who created everything that has been created, this courtesy is readily extended to the visitors who claim to be from outer space. They are generally never doubted because of the way they present themselves and the manner in which they communicate to humans.

While God is fully open to our turning to Him, these other beings pretend that it is only those who seek *within* that will find the higher knowledge that humanity supposedly seeks. The human being must be open to receiving their messages, because they cannot simply force their message on people.

God *forced* His message onto people, through the life of the very precious God, the Son. Because God did things out in the open – living among us, working among us, dying among us and rising from the dead among us – His Word means nothing to most people. He is doubted, vilified, impugned, cursed, hated, and reviled. Interesting, is it not?

The very God who loves us, gave His life for us, did it *publicly*. He is rejected. These beings who come in *secret* and give us nothing except platitudes and intelligent sounding religious dialogue, are accepted with open arms. Go figure. Such is the deceptive illusion introduced by beings from the spiritual realms, and foisted upon naive human beings.

Chapter 7
Hey, Hey We're the Monkees!

The Pleiadians told Shapiro that humans are *not* in any way connected to the monkey or the ape. While these beings have no problem discounting the results of scientific working hypotheses, they also have no problem instantly elevating man to the level of *deity*.

The Pleiadians also reflect some of the same narrative that has been out there from other spiritual entities. We were engineered through genetics. Though our true purposes have been hidden deep within the recesses of our cellular make-up, it *is* latently there and waits to be revealed. They like to call this "*divine engineering*."[26] How quaint. At every turn, Pleiadians attempt to remove a personal God from the picture, preferring instead to hand the reins of deity to man himself.

Energy, Frequencies, and Light

The Pleiadians love to talk of *energy, frequencies*, and *light*. Try to imagine if you can, what you would feel like if some entity came to you and began speaking of the mysteries of the universe. Would you not feel *special*? Would you not feel as though you were supremely important? Would you ever doubt what you heard?

The truth of the matter is that Shapiro did not doubt the message. The Pleiadians spoke to her of the energy and frequency of all *matter*. They explained how these ripples of energy could *appear* to be a solid rock, yet by manipulating the ripples of energy, the rock can disappear from one place, and appear in another. Of course, they relate that they do not expect Shapiro to understand, but in time, she will grasp more and more.

They take the time to reveal to her the job that she has been chosen to accomplish. *"Your job is twofold. Since you are an extension of Light, coming from the Creator at the beginning, you shine like a beacon throughout all of time. You will open up portals of energies that are closed or have been closed. Once these* ***portals are open****, the Darkness will not be allowed to enter, for this domain is totally yours and* ***gateways will be created that lead to other dimensions****. Nothing harmful will be allowed into these other places, only more and more Light will come until it spreads like a shimmering cover over all."*[27] (emphasis added)

Portals were discussed in my previous book *Demons in Disguise*, and they appear to be just that; portals that connect our world to the

---

[26] Lia Shapiro *Comes the Awakening* (Star Street Press, 2000), 27

[27] Ibid, 59

spiritual realms. Do they exist? Who can know? We can guess, or *choose to believe* that they exist, but it is difficult to prove from Scripture, though there may be clues.

Apparently, according to the Pleiadians, the reason they need more and more of these portals opened up is because as each new portal opens, it allegedly allows more light to flow through them, so also do the Pleiadians themselves become flooded with this light. Their goal to is become fully saturated with pure light, as the beings *above* them are so permeated. Gee, who could these Nephilim demons *possibly* be referring to here? Of course, you have also noticed how they have reversed things so that *they* are the light, and anything opposed to them is *darkness*.

Their utmost desire is to "in-lighten" us, as they tell Shapiro on page 64 of her book. Though they have tried throughout her life in particular to get her attention, there were too many times when she either did not hear them, or ignored them. However, because the Pleiadians are so inherently patient and one would almost say, *loving*, they continued, persevering in the face of the potential of complete extinction of all that dwells on earth.

What becomes actually annoying is how often the Pleiadians come right out and deny the truth of Scripture, and they are not questioned by Shapiro. "*We would like to tell you that, yes, God still does speak to people in their hearts and not only through books. There are many that quote scripture upon scripture from the Bible, or from other Holy books, believing they are speaking God's mind. Yes, they may be doing just that, but others are also. Know that God, the Ultimate Spirit and your Creator, created you, and still lives and speaks as one spirit through you. By closing off your mind to the voice of God, you shut out much information that is vital to your evolvement. Again, we must warn you at this point that all the voices you may hear within you, and even outside yourself are not the voice of your Ultimate Creator. There are many voices.*"[28] The Pleiadians do not stop there, as they explain how to know the difference between the good voices and the bad ones.

"You may ask, how is it that you will know the true one? As Children of Light, you will always know the truth. It is those creations which are not of the Light that will have difficulty. They will make mistakes and they will flounder. They will search for answers within and without, but will never really find that which they seek in this lifetime."[29]

Ultimately, of course, the Pleiadians are trying to undo all that Christianity may have done in Shapiro's mind. It obviously will not do to have a Pleiadian follower pulled in two different directions, so it is important to negate (or at the very least, *cast doubt on*), aspects of Christian thought, which may continue to lie deep within Shapiro's mind.

The Pleiadians go on to explain that Shapiro will know when she has met someone who is from *darkness*, as opposed to light. These people will tell her that her dreams and visions are evil and wrong. They will try to squelch her curiosity with respect to learning more from the Pleiadians. These people must be avoided at all costs. So it is the authentic Christian who tries to pull people like Shapiro away from this deception that she believes in, who will be seen as narrow, wrong, evil, afraid, confining and all the rest.

The Pleiadians continue, chiding and castigating authentic Christians (referring to them as "Holy" men and women), stating that these individuals are themselves deceived. These of course, should also be avoided. If Shapiro listens to her inner self, she will intuitively know the truth. Note how the Pleiadians have created pity for Christians.

If it was not tragically sad, it would be humorous, the way in which the Pleiadians even refer to themselves (Nephilim demons) as "lesser

[28] Lia Shapiro *Comes the Awakening* (Star Street Press, 2000), 66
[29] Ibid, 66

gods." Of course, to Shapiro, they are not referring to themselves, but pointing out *other* beings. In reality, they *are* referring to themselves, but how would Shapiro know that, since it is clear she doubts *not one word* spoken to her by the Pleiadians Nephilim demons.

"What you should know at this point is that many of the Lesser God are troubled. Yes, we call them gods, and their images have been fashioned from many substances and their shapes and forms exist all over the world. You may see them even in children's cartoons and toys. In many countries around the world, ancient people worshiped these gods. Even today they continue to make their likenesses. As these ugly reptilian and birdlike creatures represent the lesser evil gods, please know they are ultimately not the Supreme God at all, but they did and still do give birth to their own creations."[30]

Shapiro is then told that these beings continue to exist, yet they normally appear in human form. In short, the Pleiadians pretend that they are on the side of the true Light (as God is light), yet in reality, they are of course, *darkness*. It is interesting how much these spiritual entities wind up giving away to Shapiro. As they tell her, this information in the wrong hands could create major problems for them, but they want to take that chance because of how important Shapiro (and others like her) is for *them*.

Reading through this book reminds me of the time I went through a phase where I thought I could be captain of my own fate. It was during the time between the point of my conversion and when I had lost faith in my ability to know what was true about God or the Bible. During this period, I succumbed to the temptation to begin reading what were called *self-help books*. This was in the very early 1980s and the concept of New Age books had not really come completely to the fore, so these books, while they were being printed, fell under the self-help category of the bookstores.

[30] Lia Shapiro *Comes the Awakening* (Star Street Press, 2000), 69

A found a number of books by a man named Maxwell Maltz. At the time, I was not aware that his background was in cosmetic surgery. I only knew him as the "psycho-cybertics" guy. I purchased two of his books dealing with this subject, which was said to allow the individual to control the circumstances of their own life and existence.

For me, the time I spent with Maltz' books was not long at all. Looking back, I realize that his books were every bit eastern mystical as the books that claim to be eastern mystical today. He spoke of controlling your own destiny through *out of body* experiences, sending thought waves, and patterns to control situations, people, or both.

Yep, I was a regular New Ager myself, or becoming one at that point, but fortunately for me, God squashed that very quickly, by creating a real boredom within toward these methods. I do remember at one point, going through the motions of trying to "soul travel," and while lying on my bed, instead of falling asleep, as I would normally have done, the thoughts and images in my brain became more vivid than I had ever experienced. Normally, in sleep, we can often have very vivid dreams, some so real that we wake up with a start from them. I was beginning to experience that then, while lying on my bed, with my eyes wide open! After having pulled away from that whole arena and realizing what continued experimentation *might* have resulted in, I confessed my sin to the Lord, and He cleansed me from it. The only time I look at books like that now, is for research while writing one of my own.

Good Vibrations

Pleiadians taught Shapiro that the proper *vibrations* will increase a person's receptivity to light. The more light a person has, the less they will fear. Antiquated religions (like Christianity), create fear of God in people. Because of this, more light is lost and darkness takes over. These individuals wind up not being able to have an original thought apparently. The idea is that the more light a person absorbs, the more that person is truly free from darkness. The freer they are from darkness, the less they will fear God, evil, or other things. It is fear that keeps people bound apparently. Never mind that the Bible tells us throughout that we should *fear* God and as my pastor says, "Fearing God means *fearing* God!"

Even believers should fear God. This is more than having a healthy respect or reverence for someone or something. When John saw Jesus in the book of Revelation, he crumbled to the ground because of his own uncleanness. Ezekiel also, as well as numerous other prophets of men of God, experienced this same type of fear and feelings of wretchedness.

Because we are believers, this does not automatically remove our sin nature. It still exists, as does our corrupt flesh, *until* we see Christ in the next life. When we do, we will be like Him, according to John. Fearing God because of who He is, and the absolute power He wields is something that *should* be the normal existence of every authentic believer.

Of course, the Pleiadians tell us the exact *opposite* of this. Ultimately, they want human beings to open the doors of their heart and mind to *them*, which will grant them greater access to the affairs of this world. The greater number of human beings who give them access, the greater their collective ability to control not only the lives of those humans, but the events and situations in this world, because they will be doing it essentially from *within* people, even if they do not wind up possessing them directly. It could include possession, but might also simply occur through manipulation of thoughts and beliefs. In effect, the people who are motivated this way will be doing things of their own volition, which makes it easier for the Nephilim demons. In that way, they will have access to the person's thoughts and feelings and because of that, they will be able to exercise an overall control of that person's life and the lives of the people they touch.

The Pleiadians are insistent on a number of things, which they tend to repeat to Shapiro. They need her to be a *willing participant in,* and *receptacle of,* the information and "truth" they provide her. Once they gain anyone's trust, the rest if smooth sailing, if and until such a point when their actual identities and motives are seen by the individual who has placed their trust in them.

Already Here

Besides the constant discussion of *light, light energy,* and *frequencies,* the other valuable insight that the Pleiadians push is the alleged fact that there are already living among us are "*actual planetary beings living among [us].*"[31] Of course, who knows if this is true? While it is easy enough to espouse, it is difficult if not impossible to prove, and of course, the Pleiadians are not interested in proving anything. That would mean that they are admitting that the people they are disseminating their message *to* and *through* might have a difficult time believing them.

There are many on the Internet who firmly believe that there are beings known as the Reptilians, as well as other species, which have taken on the *form* of humanity. They do this so that they might blend in with humans, without being discovered.

The folks on the 'Net point to their videos, photos, and eyewitness testimony to prove that these beings do in fact, exist and are living among us. To most, this will seem to be directly from a Men in Black movie (from which the origins goes back to the 1950s in some form or another).

Some of the videos are interesting, some are unexplainable, and yet others are unintentionally funny, simply because it appears as though the people who posted the video are trying desperately to see something in the video that is not there. One video was placed up on

[31] Lia Shapiro *Comes the Awakening* (Star Street Press, 2000), 111

the 'Net boasting the video capture of a weird beast of sorts. The problem was, that the folks who put the video up, forgot to include the "beast," which they were apparently going to drop in later.

The video was shot, with people acting extremely afraid, and the videographer used quick, shaky camera movements (ala Blair Witch Project), but there was nothing to see through the viewfinder, except empty background. The actors were certainly *acting* as if there was something there, however. That was funny!

The reality though is that more and more people accept the belief that these beings do exist and they are among us already. The reason they are here – according to the Pleiadians – is uniquely related to that particular entity. Some are good, some are not so good, and others are pure evil Shapiro was told. How will the person who believes the Pleiadians know the difference? The internal whisperings of the person's own being will set it straight on that score.

Repeatedly, the Pleiadians simply say things like "*understand we come for good purposes*," or "*know that we come in love*," etc. Because they say it, it must be true, so no need to ask them for verification. No worries, because to date, my research has not found anyone who actually *has* taken the time to ask for verification of their intentions.

It is unfortunate that page after page of Shapiro's book is simply more of the same ethereal jargon and verbiage, designed to put our fears at rest, while taking advantage of our collective gullibility. Taken by themselves, many of the things the Pleiadians speak of, espouse, and encourage us to do are *absurd*.

We can fly, for instance, though we have simply not yet liberated that part of ourselves. We must do things like this *slowly*, so that over time, this will become an adaptable ability, adaptable to our particular circumstances. We should never limit ourselves. So what if somebody who is slightly off takes this part of it too fast, and kills themselves as they jump off the roof of a building? Does it matter? No, simply because their being will be recycled (read: *reincarnated*) back through the entire system of life. Besides, if someone *does* try this and dies, the Pleiadians do not have to worry about being sued by remaining family members.

Frankly, continuing to read Shapiro's book creates a sense of monotony within, namely because the same ideas and concepts are expressed repeatedly, though with different verbiage. By the time chapter thirteen begins, the phrase "*you are one*" has been stated too many times to count.

Chapter 8
Don't Fear the Reaper

Interestingly, while many New Agers read Shapiro's book and shout a big "WOW!", I find it difficult to continue reading without four cups of coffee, just to keep from falling asleep. So much of what is espoused by these "higher beings" is mundane, yet to the uninitiated, the very words these Pleiadians speak are life itself. Of course, these people need God, yet until they are willing to reach for Him, they will remain in their darkness.

One of the big secrets to finding out many things about the universe is to seek it from within your spirit. At one point, the Pleiadians described Shapiro as a *"ball of Light bouncing through time, riding the*

Cosmic Wave. The Light that you are is the Spirit of all *that you are. What you think you are, you are not at all."*[32] Unbelievably awe-inspiring, isn't it? Such depth. Such grandiose imagery. Imagine, what I think I am, I am not. What I *do* not think I am, that I am. Wow. These guys could write a book. Oh wait, they did.

Truth is Within

They continue focusing on the person's spirit by stating, "*The key to accessing your Spirit lies within you* (surprise! – ed.). *All you have to do now is begin to turn the key. Dare to walk through the door of your spiritual mind and see what is on the other side. As you allow yourself to peer into this new world, you will begin to remember that which you originated from. You will begin to see that you are not solid and rigid at all like you once perceived yourself to be* (this is due to the waves of energy that they say makes up all solids – ed.). *Even your dramas that you participate in are not as solid as you may think them to be. Your Spirit originates with the highest frequency, which is the ultimate frequency, and which is the Creator of all. You begin with God and ride through time like a never ending, golden thread of Light. You unravel throughout eternity, twisting, touching and zigzagging in and out of what you call realities, or lives."*[33]

What is particularly special about the loving concern of the Pleiadians is that they are willing to be so helpful. "*We will help you to turn the key and unlock secrets. It is then when you will begin to truly know and understand that there is no such thing as death. How can death possibly exist when your Spirit so obviously traverses the Cosmos with such joy, abandonment and freedom? The Spirit is never ending. Know this to be true without doubt. The Spirit* never *dies. It is as free as the wind. As you think you die, know that the Spirit is leaping and springing forth from the shackles of human bondage instead. There is never ending joy to its final escape into that which it came.*

[32] Lia Shapiro *Comes the Awakening* (Star Street Press, 2000), 142
[33] Ibid, 143

This is the true home from which we all were created, and from which we all will continue to reside in."[34]

It is clear that the Pleiadians have it seriously goin' on. I mean think of it. In one swell swoop, they have swept the truth of the Bible off the table, and no one asks them why. Their word is accepted as gospel. In fact, messages like those from the Pleiadians *are* the new gospel, because it is all-inclusive and eliminates *rules, regulations,* and *God's moral law.*

Unlike the truth of Scripture and the gospel found therein, the gospel of the Pleiadians teaches that we go from great to *greater,* to *greatest!* Who would not be excited about that? It is difficult to continue to read their words without wanting to offer sarcastic rejoinders and asides in response to their "truth." The most difficult aspect of everything is when it is clear that they *are* telling the truth (*"Nothing is by accident, and nothing is hurled randomly into the Earth realm. All is by careful choice and by expert planning," page 143 – ed.),* though they act as if it is *their* truth, when it is clearly God's truth!

Rearranging Your Molecular Structure

Apparently, according to the Pleiadians, it is imperative that our molecules become rearranged. Sounds exciting. Are you excited? I am excited. While this may at first sound difficult (or even ridiculous), once understood, it becomes quite an easy thing to achieve apparently. The letdown though is that while it will become relatively easy to rearrange these *"tiny round balls,"*[35] the truth of the matter, is that it will not be noticeable except over *time,* as we continue to evolve and change.

Since curiosity killed the cat, the Pleiadians answer the unasked question by stating, *"It is important that you understand how these internal changes will not be seen, but they will definitely be felt. As*

[34] Lia Shapiro *Comes the Awakening* (Star Street Press, 2000), 143
[35] Ibid, 145

your DNA structure code is changed, you will change. As your nervous system is changed, you will also be changed. Many systems will begin to alter. As a result, you may experience so called symptoms of many kinds. These symptoms are really only a minor annoyance compared to the final and glorious overhaul of your entire system. We hope to give you assurance by telling you that it is possible that you will only grow better as the years go by. In fact, some will marvel that you do not seem to age or deteriorate as others do."[36]

Death will seem to be going backwards? Huh, interesting. It is possible to heal ourselves. I don't know about you, but I am quite satisfied with that explanation. In fact, it warms the cockles of my heart to have this information.

By the time the Pleiadians get to chapter fourteen, they really start to open up with Shapiro. As usual, it always comes down to religion. *"Religion as you know it will* ***blind you to the absolute truth****. Understand that what we tell you will open you up to encompass all of God as God was meant to be known...As we have mentioned before, God is neither a he nor a she, but is frequency existing at the highest order."*[37] (emphasis added)

From this point, it appears as though they have Shapiro right where they want her and begin to zero in on her world view like never before, continuing to burst one long held bubble after another. Though they continue to issue their warnings and information with the same worn out phrases they have been using since chapter one, in some ways, it almost always appears to be *new*, as if this the first time they have made these statements. In truth, they appear to be using a form of hypnosis, by constantly repeating the same phrases, though including a new phrase here and there amidst the same information.

---

[36] Lia Shapiro *Comes the Awakening* (Star Street Press, 2000), 146
[37] Ibid, 149

In this way, they are not shocking the person who reads Shapiro's book. They are simply *expanding* ever so slightly the information that they began providing 150 pages ago. This allows the novice as well as the more ardent New Age practitioner to come along at their own speed. You see, there is nothing to fear from the Pleiadians.

The overall picture that they are trying to present is that we "*are all trapped in a web of lies and deceit, for [we] believe that without money all is hopeless. And indeed it is because you are like a small snowball that rolls and rolls and becomes bigger until finally it is huge. This is how money is. We tell you that you will never make enough and you will never have enough. You will make more, and more, and more, but you will only keep spending more as the snowball grows.*"[38] One wonders if the Pleiadians ever submitted their resumes to teach economics at some of the Ivy League schools. Obviously, their talents are wasted.

The upshot of course, is that they are not simply giving this short course on economics for the sake of it. This, like everything else they talk about, is leading to something. What they say they want is for our earthly society to be built on *love* and *trust*. In this regard, the foundation for such a society is found in human *relationships*, not money. If we could all simply let go of money, then society the world over would flourish.

Interestingly enough, as we move toward a one-world order, comprised of a one-world government and a one-world religion, it should be noted that life at that point would probably be reflected in our economics by a one-world monetary system. If there is a one-world currency, then there is no reason for one nation to be pitted against another nation, to gain and maintain the highest value for their particular currency over against the currencies of other countries.

[38] Lia Shapiro *Comes the Awakening* (Star Street Press, 2000), 154

In spite of the fact that they just finished telling us that "religion will blind us to the absolute truth," on page 146, they come back roughly 15 to 20 pages later with "*Religion offers hope, perhaps with a prize or reward in the end.*"[39]

So which is it – does religion *blind us,* or does it *offer hope*? Is the correct answer *both*? You tell me, because it does not appear as though the Pleiadians are telling us.

[39] Lia Shapiro *Comes the Awakening* (Star Street Press, 2000), 163

Chapter 9

The Power of Love

When it all comes down to it, the Pleiadians delight to tell us that there is nothing more important than *love* as previously discussed. They repeat it often enough to Shapiro. It is the most important thing primarily because it unleashes *power.*

How do they *define* love though? First, it begins in the spiritual realm and connects to our *emotions* or *feelings.* Love is the only thing. There is nothing else truer, more pure, or more powerful.

On the heels of this, they then tell us that staying with an individual in marriage for a lifetime just might not be the best idea. It can actually be stunting. The reason for this has to do with the fact that as we grow, we are constantly learning what love is, and what love is not. Because of this, we may enter into a relationship with someone during a certain understanding of love, yet as we grow, our married partner does not grow with us. Because of that, we are not enabled to love as we are meant to love. In such a case, looking for a more suitable person is for the better.

More Relationships Lead to More Love
"Understand that it is through relationships that you will comprehend Love. It is here that you will grow and develop and remember that from which you came. It is in Love that you can have and be everything, even though you may have nothing else at all."[40] Such depth. Could Shakespeare have said it any better?

The ironic thing about the Pleiadians is that regardless of how much truth they offer, or how many times they offer it, they always acknowledge that we are not able to fully comprehend it. In fact, there is so much more that they *wish* to reveal to us, but in our current state, it is impossible to do so. *Sigh...*

They head off into the area of uncovering truth, which can come through many forms. They speak of the many different religious belief systems and while they remain disjointed and even at odds one with another, they are really all pieces of the same pizza. That is good to know, isn't it? Whew, what a load off my mind!

They explain that the reason there are so many different systems is due to the fact that people are all at different places, different levels of energy receptivity. Because of this, what appear to be contradictions

---

[40] Lia Shapiro *Comes the Awakening* (Star Street Press, 2000), 181

between religious thought are nothing more than different *ends* of the same line.

They do take the time to point out that though we have all heard the terms "sinner," or "sinful," or similar, and that we need forgiveness, the real truth of the matter is that we *"are already forgiven because there is nothing to forgive. The God you believe in lives inside of you, and* ***is*** *you!"*[41] (emphasis added)

Aha! Caught Them!

Though they tell us that all religions are essentially different points of the same path, which presumably lead to the same ultimate goal (or *end*), they *then* turn around and intone, *"there is no one truth."*[42] I suppose the fact that these two concepts are separated by over 20 pages, leads them to think that you will either not remember what they said earlier, or you will think that you must not be understanding it correctly. In either case, the fault will lie at your door.

If you were to ask the Pleiadians about this (and other) apparent contradictions, they might respond as so, *"Ah, what you have experienced is what we call a burble in the linear wavelength. This has a tendency to make you believe that two things are in contradiction to one another, when in reality, they are merely two sides of the same coin. In this case, we are referring to the Susan B. Anthony dollar. You may have wondered why that particular coin was ever minted by what you refer to as your government.*

"The reasons for this will become apparent as time (and remember, there is no such thing as time, though we refer to time because it is a term that is familiar to you), moves in a slightly linear fashion toward the planet Sirius in the Komadi constellation. That would be the fourth planet just to the right of Never, Never Land, if you were to look through a high-powered electron telescope.

---

[41] Lia Shapiro *Comes the Awakening* (Star Street Press, 2000), 185

[42] Ibid, 212

"Know that contradictions only appear to be contradictions because this is what you have programmed yourself to believe about things that seem to be against one another, one truth attempting by its existence to cancel out another truth. Of course, this is impossible because since there is no one truth, truths cannot oppose one another, but only complement one another. We wish you were able to fully and consciously absorb all that we teach, but alas, the complexity of our teaching and the shallowness of your brainwaves and patterns preclude such a conclusion.

"Please do not be offended as we wish only the best for you. Know that in time, all things that seem to contradict will be understood as they are, without the slightest sense of contradiction."

Of course, by the time they get to their second paragraph, you are lost because they are merely speaking gobbledygook. Because they *sound* intelligent, they are convincing. Besides, who wants to admit that they do not understand what the Pleiadians are teaching? The words are English, but it is nonsensical. By the way, this is what the average individual reading Shapiro's book misses. Shapiro *heard* these beings presenting this information to her, as other channellers heard the information presented to them. The tone in which these concepts were presented is absent from the book, so the individual reader creates that tone in their own minds.

The last chapter – twenty-one – focuses on the awakening that is desired to take place within each person. It is here that they also present an excuse as to why they are unable to explain things so that they will be clearly understood. Never mind that they are deliberately speaking nonsense, though intelligent *sounding* nonsense, mixing actual truth with their error. The fault lies with the *words* themselves. "*Speaking of words,"* says the Pleiadians, "*we can find them terribly limiting. If we could apply our* own words, *things would go much better, if only you knew our language. We will not go into the details of our language, as it really serves no purpose at this point. Simply know that we can speak any language, but that our language gives a more expanded and detailed view in much less words, or with no words at all!"*[43]

Of course, you see what they have done. They have answered a question before it was ever asked. While they introduce the idea that their language is so much more rich, they quickly negate the use of it by stating that there is no need to discuss their language because it serves no purpose. If that is so, then why bring it up in the first place? Beyond that, didn't the Pleiadians spend the past 200 plus pages explaining that we are already *god*? Because we are already *god* are we not able to fly, rearrange our molecular DNA, and manipulate solid matter (which is not really solid at all)? Okay then, why can't we learn their language, especially if they are already *part* of us, and dwell *within* us and we in *them*?

I guess no one bothered to ask them that. Well, I am asking, and the answer *is* because these Nephilim demons and fallen angels are filled to the brim with excrement. Though they sound like eternal sages to the uninformed, they are nothing but fallen angels and demons in space alien attire.

With their smooth words, they flatter and scratch itching ears. They continue to shovel it on, spinning their web of lies and deceit until they have not only caught their prey, but also securely spun their web of death around them until the victim is unable to move one way or another. From there it is a matter of slowly draining the victim of life until they are completely taken over by the "Pleiadian."

Some of the inane statements they make are laughable except for the fact that they have hypnotized their victim to the point of being unable to resist. Like Jeffrey Dahmer or John Wayne Gacy, who gained the trust of their victims with their friendliness and outgoing

---

[43] Lia Shapiro *Comes the Awakening* (Star Street Press, 2000), 222

demeanor, or by being able to offer the victim something they did not have, so too do the Nephilim demons and fallen angels come to human beings as the innocent, caring, loving, patient and kind Pleiadians. They begin to spin their deceitful web, providing a bit of information here and a bit more there. As time goes on, the victim lowers all defenses until the Pleiadians can say just about anything and the hearer will accept it without thought or concern.

Here are some of the insightful statements made by the Pleiadians:

- *"When your soul arrived on Earth in the form of a newborn baby, your perceptions were not as they are now."*[44] Really? Who would have thought that? Not me.
- *"Look into the eyes of a newborn and you can plainly see that the spirit comes and goes."*[45] Umm, I thought that was called *sleep.*
- *"You will suffer, you will feel pain and experience joy."* Now, *there's* some good news!

Are these statements not insightful? Their final comment on page 233 is *"It is* you *that will continue to seek that which you need, here and now, and forever more."*[46] Frankly, I was hoping they would end with something like, "To Infinity, and Beyond!"

I mean, whom are we kidding? Most of Shapiro's book is an exercise in being obsequious. The Pleiadians spend most of the time trying to make human beings feel good about themselves, and even when they "must" say something that could be construed as offensive, they are quick to apologize, stating that their intent is not to offend, but to teach and instruct. However, what is it they have actually taught human beings? It can be summed up in three statements:

---

[44] Lia Shapiro *Comes the Awakening* (Star Street Press, 2000), 231
[45] Ibid, 231
[46] Ibid, 233

1. *We are God*
2. *We create our own reality*
3. *Love is the most important thing in the universe*

I know I'm not the first one to say this, as I have read what I'm about to say in Chuck Missler's books as well as others, but *if* they are so truly concerned about us and our welfare, as they claim to be, why have they not provided *anything* that will actually *improve* society at the physical level?

By their own admission, they are light years ahead of us, yet they share nothing about eliminating the very things that keep us *bound* to the physical:

- *AIDS*
- *Famines*
- *Diseases of all kinds*
- *Undrinkable water*
- *A place to put our garbage, or a way to recycle ALL of it*
- *Problem of crime*
- *Problem of hatred and racism*

I am sure you could add other things to the above list and so could I. Why are they not helping with any of those things? They seem completely uninterested in assisting us eliminate sicknesses and famines. They are not telling us how to purify the water throughout the globe, or how to recycle all of the things we throw out, so that absolutely nothing is wasted. Beyond this, they do not seem at all motivated to help us take a bite out of crime, working right alongside McGruff! Coupled with that is the problem of hatred that is often based on ethnicity and race, which exists throughout this world.

The Pleiadians are very willing to help us see our own deity, but they are sure tight lipped about these other areas, aren't they? Makes me wonder why they bother, especially when they state repeatedly throughout Shapiro's book that we will be learning, growing, and evolving for an *eternity*. I guess at some point, because we are god, we will eventually figure out how to eradicate the diseases that are making people drop like flies every day. Of course, we have to master the art of flying first, so that we can flit from one end of the universe to the other, traversing layers and layers that are built into the fabric of our universe.

That also leads to a similar question regarding Shapiro herself. During one of her early experiences in which she traveled the universe and came in contact with "God," why did she only come back to earth with *feelings*? She really had no new knowledge at all, certainly nothing she could share that would change the physical problems in this world. It was all based on experience, stemming from overpowering feelings she experienced. How does that help anyone? It does not, because all it directs people to do is go *inward* to search for truth.

In India, when someone reaches a state or level of experience (or is it *existence*?) in which they are called a *spiritual master,* or *enlightened master*, in some cases the individuals have become catatonic. There they sit, with people around them needing to do everything for them including washing them helping them eat and drink, etc. It is ridiculous, yet it is venerated as some form of spiritually enlightened state. This is tragic, yet this is what Nephilim demons, and fallen angels can ultimately lead people to experience.

Chapter 10
Three Steps to Heaven

Lia Shapiro presents the information she learned from the Pleiadians, as a matter of indisputable fact, as though what she shares should be common knowledge for everyone. She assumes a great deal, that the Pleiadians are *real* entities, as space aliens, and not Nephilim demons or fallen angels.

She speaks of soaring through the various layers of the universe as if on Aladdin's magic carpet, and during that time, mysteries of the universe were revealed to her. Unfortunately, these particular mysteries are all relegated to the area of *religious* thought. The emotions of love, joy, and peace were hers to experience. Apart from her emotions though, what did she actually *learn* about the universe? She learned *nothing*, nothing at all. She gained no insight into anything outside of herself and anything she was *told* was simply presented to her as fact, and she never took the time to question any of it.

On the other hand, what do *we* know about the universe? Does the Bible say anything, or must we rely only on science? Even the Pleiadians do not rely on science to explain the expanse and mystery of the universe. They rely on *feeling*, and *experience* to teach what they know.

Fortunately, the very Creator of the universe itself goes much further in providing insight into the truths of the universe. These truths are understandable, and they come to us from the very Word of God.

The Bible, Geology & Genesis

Recently, in researching for this book, I happened upon a wonderful article by a man named Gaines Johnson, who is a Christian Geologist. His article titled, "**The Firmament, Third Heaven, and Structure of Things Biblical**," is excellent in many respects (soon to be released as a book, with many other connected articles). I do not believe it was by accident that I happened on his page and specifically this article. I wrote him, asking for permission to quote a good portion of it and he was kind enough to extend me that courtesy.

The reason I am including a good portion of his article here is that he explains *from Scripture*, what God has revealed to us regarding the mysterious phrase, *the Firmament*. There have been many articles written on the subject of the firmament, with most authors unable to come to any solid conclusions regarding the nature of the firmament and its actual *purpose*. Mr. Johnson's article struck me for its *clarity* and I did not feel like an idiot as I read it. Johnson obviously knows about that which he speaks, and is able to make it simple enough for people like myself who do not have a background in science to understand it.

When I had finished reading it, so many things simply fell into place. I cannot thank him enough for putting his thoughts to paper, as it were. I would encourage each reader to avail himself or herself of the information on Mr. Johnson's website, as there are many articles all equally well done. I have recreated the images in Photoshop® that were on his site, based on the design of those images. Mr. Johnson retains all copyrights to this original article, and you will find his unedited copy in italics. When he quotes Scripture, it normally follows his comments. I greatly appreciate his willingness to allow me to reprint it here. There are more articles on his website: ***http://www.kjvbible.org/firmament.html***

The Firmament

We know that the Creation is explained to us in Genesis chapter one. We know that God refers to 24-hour periods of time, which many take to mean *eons* of time. If that was the case though, there would have been no need for God to qualify the word "day" with 24-hours. The fact that the narrative includes the 24-hour references indicates that what God meant was that He portioned up Creation into actual *days,* measured in periods of 24-hours each.

The man who wrote the article to which I refer and from which I draw information references Genesis 1:6-8, which states, "*And God said, Let there be a firmament in the midst of the waters, and let it divide the waters from the waters. And God made the firmament, and divided the waters which were under the firmament from the waters which were above the firmament: and it was so. And God called the firmament Heaven. And the evening and the morning were the second day,*" (KJV).

Of this, Johnson indicates, "*On the second day in the Genesis narrative, the Lord calls for there to be a "firmament" in the "midst of the waters" to divide the waters,"*[47] Johnson goes on to point out that in these verses, it is clear that God created something called a "firmament." Of this, Johnson states, "*The term "firmament" and its identity has been one of the greatest puzzles concerning the Creation account, mostly because of its Hebrew definition:*

" Strongs Hebrew Definition # 7549: eyqr raqiya` raw-kee'-ah from 7554; properly, an expanse, i.e. the firmament or (apparently) visible arch of the sky:--firmament.

"Strongs Hebrew Definition # 7554: eqr raqa` raw-kah' a primitive root; to pound the earth (as a sign of passion); by analogy to expand (by hammering); by implication, to overlay (with thin sheets of metal):--beat, make broad, spread abroad (forth, over, out, into plates), stamp, stretch."[48]

I remember reading books and commentaries by numerous individuals who could not state for certain just exactly what a firmament is in actuality. Even Chuck Missler stated, "*The word 'firmament' is a problem. What is the firmament? Nobody knows. What are the waters? Nobody knows."*[49] Because of that, numerous definitions, or attempts to explain the meaning of the firmament exist.

Frankly, I have yet to read a better understanding of it than Johnson's. He states, "*Most people interpret this to mean just the expanse of the sky (the atmosphere) or outer space, or both (which it is), but the full meaning goes well beyond that simplistic*

---

[47] http://www.kjvbible.org/firmament.html

[48] http://www.kjvbible.org/firmament.html

[49] Chuck Missler *Learn the Bible in Twenty-Four Hours* (Nashville: Thomas Nelson), 16

interpretation. The creation of the firmament is associated with the placement of some sort of structure."[50]

This is exactly how theologians normally present the firmament. I think that Johnson has a bit of a leg up on this because of his background in geology. He continues, "*Many modern scholars consign the term 'firmament' as a relic of a pre-scientific culture and translate the Hebrew word "raqia" (rendered as 'firmament' in the KJV) as a 'dome' or 'vault' in some modern Bibles. The problem that puzzles people is the implication in the Hebrew language of the firmament being a firm, fixed structure (FIRMament). That structure can be explained in the context of the Ruin-Reconstruction interpretation of Genesis."*[51]

Another point that Johnson addresses is connected to the firmament. It has to do with the waters, which at one time are said to have surrounded the earth *externally*. He explains it this way, "*Young Earth Creationists have interpreted the 'waters above the firmament' as a theoretical water canopy, which once surrounded the Earth but no longer exists (their source of the waters of Noah's flood). This is incorrect, and a concept that does not exactly hold water (pun intended) when closely examined within the literal framework of the Genesis narrative. The reason is due to what is stated in this passage:*

'And God said, Let there be lights in the firmament of the heaven to divide the day from the night; and let them be for signs, and for seasons, and for days, and years: And let them be for lights in the firmament of the heaven to give light upon the earth: and it was so. And God made two great lights; the greater light to rule the day, and the lesser light to rule the night: he made the stars also.' (Genesis 1:14-16)"[52]

---

[50] http://www.kjvbible.org/firmament.html
[51] http://www.kjvbible.org/firmament.html
[52] Ibid

Frankly, if not for Johnson's understanding here, these verses would still be slightly confusing. I am grateful to him for his ability to understand what God has described here. Johnson explains it by saying, "*This verse says that the Sun, Moon, and Stars are IN the firmament. Therefore, applying the rules of grammar and logic, those waters that are above the firmament must be above the Sun, Moon, and Stars. That means these waters are above the visible cosmos. For some this is a hard pill to swallow, but that is exactly what the Bible is saying.*"[53] The Scripture from Psalms 148:4 is then referenced by Johnson, which reads, "*Praise him, ye heavens of heavens, and ye waters that [be] above the heavens,*"[54] (KJV).

What has always been a bit difficult for me to comprehend is the way in which the universe has been created. Is there a structure to it? If so, what is that structure?

Johnson believes he understands that Scripture teaches that there *is* a specific structure to the universe. "*The Bible says that in the Lord Jesus Christ, the incarnate Word of God, all wisdom and knowledge is found (see Colossians 2:3). The same holds true for the Holy Scriptures, the written Word of God. According to the Scriptures, there is a physical/spiritual structure to the universe. The Apostle Paul refers to the importance of this knowledge in the book of Ephesians where he wrote:*

"That Christ may dwell in your hearts by faith; that ye, being rooted and grounded in love, May be able to comprehend with all saints what [is] the breadth, and length, and depth, and height; And to know the love of Christ, which passeth knowledge, that ye might be filled with all the fulness of God." (Ephesians 3:17-19)"[55]

[53] http://www.kjvbible.org/firmament.html
[54] Ibid
[55] Ibid

In considering the Ephesians passage, do *you* know what Paul is referring to here? Admittedly, I need to read Paul's words three, four or five times before they even *begin* to make sense. Paul is as concise as he can possibly be, yet some of the concepts he espouses require a good amount of verbiage (the book of Romans for instance). Here Paul is speaking about dimensions. Is he speaking of the dimensions of the love of Christ?

"Pay close attention to the structure of the grammar. Paul is speaking about two different things in this passage. The first is the structure of things ("the breadth, and length, and depth, and height;"), and the second is 'to know the love of Christ, which passeth knowledge.' The important key word here is the conjunction 'And' which separates the two clauses.

"In other words, Paul is saying there are two things the believer can and should know. 1) The dimensions and structure of all things, which can be defined. 2) The love of Christ, which is beyond full comprehension by man. A corollary to the truth of this passage is found in an Old Testament proverb: 'The heaven for height, and the earth for depth, and the heart of kings [is] unsearchable'. (Proverbs 25:3)"[56]

Johnson further narrows things down for us. "*The firmament deals with the structure of the present heavens and Earth (Genesis 2:1), as opposed to the structure of the original heaven and Earth (Genesis 1:1). There is presently a three (3) heavens structure. In the old world of the original creation, there was a different configuration. Let's look back to Genesis 1:6 again and more closely examine that verse to determine that present structure: 'And God said, Let there be a firmament in the midst of the waters, and let it divide the waters from the waters. And God made the firmament, and divided the waters which [were] under the firmament from the waters which [were] above the firmament: and it was so'. (Genesis 1:6-7 KJV)*"

---

[56] http://www.kjvbible.org/firmament.html

If you take the time to re-read Genesis 1:6-7, it is easy to simply read it, inserting the understanding that we have come to know. Yet, in reading it closely, we can gain something more. *"On the second day of the creation, the Lord God "divided" the waters (plural) of the great "deep" into two parts with a "firmament" in the midst. According to Genesis 1:10, both the waters that were upon the face of the Earth and the waters which He placed ABOVE the firmament He called "Seas": 'And God called the dry [land] Earth; and the gathering together of the waters called he Seas: and God saw that [it was] good.' (Gen 1:10 KJV)"*[57]

Johnson calls attention to the fact that the word "Seas" is capitalized. Did you notice it? Johnson notes, "*This is important to understand. We know that the waters on the Earth are called "Seas" in the Bible, but there is also another "Sea" that is spoken of in the Scriptures, and that one is above the firmament. (Special note: Notice that the word "Sea" is capitalized at Genesis 1:10 in the KJV Bible). But, exactly where is "ABOVE" the firmament? During the six days of the Genesis regeneration the Lord God defined Three Heavens. The first heaven is the Earth's atmosphere: 'And God said, Let the waters bring forth abundantly the moving creature that hath life, and fowl [that] may fly above the earth in the open firmament of heaven.' (Genesis 1:20 KJV)"*[58]

I have always thought that the mention of Earth referenced the Earth and the word "Seas" referenced the water *on* the Earth. If so, why would God have included the word "Seas" separately? By simply mentioning the Earth, that would have included the waters that were on the Earth, making the use of the word "Seas" redundant and therefore, unnecessary.

Johnson continues, "*The second heaven is the vast expanse of the physical universe - outer space as we call it: 'And God said, Let there be*

[57] http://www.kjvbible.org/firmament.html
[58] Ibid

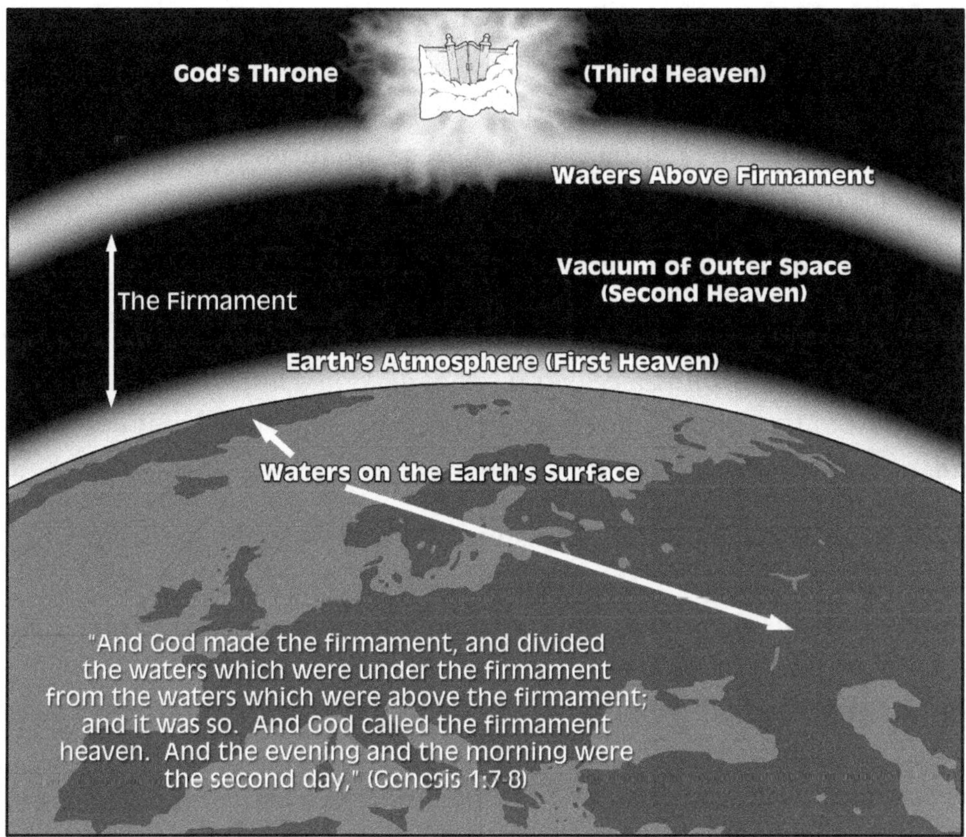

lights in the firmament of the heaven to divide the day from the night; and let them be for signs, and for seasons, and for days, and years:' (Genesis 1:14)"[59]

The illustration above highlights what Johnson refers to, and is based on the drawing that he uses on his website.

Johnson points out that "*These two heavens constitute a continuum called the "firmament," and this firmament is collectively called 'Heaven': 'And God called the firmament Heaven. And the evening and the morning were the second day.'* (Genesis 1:8)"[60]

---

[59] Ibid

[60] http://www.kjvbible.org/firmament.html

Third Heaven

We have all read where Paul speaks of a Third Heaven. Arnold G. Fruchtenbaum also references this in his book *Footsteps of the Messiah*. We get the impression that there are three separate heavens, or areas above us.

Johnson continues with, "*The Third Heaven is above this higher 'Sea,' and this higher sea is before and below the Throne of God:*

'And before the throne there was a sea of glass like unto crystal: and in the midst of the throne, and round about the throne, were four beasts full of eyes before and behind.' (Revelation 4:6)"[61]

As strange as it may sound, Johnson arrives at the only plausible conclusion to the use of the word "Seas" in this section. He says, "*Therefore, this particular "Sea" above the firmament is above the known physical universe. Since the sun, moon and stars are "in" the firmament this "Sea" MUST be above them. This is difficult for the science of man to fathom, but it is a Scriptural fact on cosmology. It represents a firm and impassable barrier between the world of man (below) and the abode of God (above). Here are some additional verses in the Bible, which refer to this particular Sea: 'Praise him, ye heavens of heavens, and ye waters that [be] above the heavens.'* (Psalms 148:4)"[62]

Are there more examples of this "sea" in other portions of Scripture, or is it just here? There are other areas, and Johnson points them out to us.

"*This is the "sea" that John saw in his visions: 'And before the throne [there was] a sea of glass like unto crystal: and in the midst of the*

---

[61] http://www.kjvbible.org/firmament.html
[62] Ibid

throne, and round about the throne, [were] four beasts full of eyes before and behind.' (Rev 4:6)"[63]

In my previous book, *Demons in Disguise*, I noted that a number of aliens when revealing things to human beings spoke of *portals*. They gain access to and from our world using these portals. The interesting thing here is that if there is a literal "Sea" above the earth, which separates us from God's throne physically, then it would make sense that portals might be necessary by beings of God's Creation in the spiritual realm. As stated in conjunction with that, the fact that Gabriel seemed to have no alternative other than to go back to God's throne by way of the Prince of Persia offers some support for this view.

Commenting on the "Sea" that he believes exists above the earth, he says, "*This is a present "Sea" of separation that will no longer exist when God destroys the old world and makes all things new after the 1,000-year Kingdom of Heaven and the final judgment that follows: 'And I saw a new heaven and a new earth: for the first heaven and the first earth were passed away; and there was no more sea.'* (Revelation 21:1)"[64]

Johnson further draws comparisons to this "Sea" from other areas in Scripture. "*This is the sea that is spoken of in Exodus 20:11 and frequently quoted by Young Earth Creationists as a proof text to support their doctrine: 'For in six days the LORD made heaven and earth, the sea, and all that in them is, and rested the seventh day: wherefore the LORD blessed the sabbath day, and hallowed it.'* (Exodus 20:11)"

Johnson believes that the "sea" in the above verse "*is a reference to the sea established above the firmament NOT to any sea on the Earth. Look at the English grammar of the verse. The heaven and Earth are*

---

[63] Ibid

[64] http://www.kjvbible.org/firmament.html

set apart as separate and complete entities as is "the sea." That sea above the firmament was not made until the second day. There is something even more important to notice about these waters above the firmament. Look again at the passage concerning the second day: "And God said, Let there be a firmament in the midst of the waters, and let it divide the waters from the waters. And God made the firmament, and divided the waters which were under the firmament from the waters which were above the firmament: and it was so. And God called the firmament Heaven. And the evening and the morning were the second day.' (Genesis 1:6-8)"[65]

Some might disagree with Johnson's assessment here. To buttress his reasoning he points out "*Something is missing there. Do you know what it is? Ok, I'll tell you. This work on the second day is the ONLY day in the Genesis narrative where the Lord does NOT say it "was good." Therefore, when you consider the statement the Lord makes in Genesis 1:31 where He says that all that was made was "very good"...'And God saw every thing that he had made, and, behold, it was very good. And the evening and the morning were the sixth day.'* (Genesis 1:31)"[66]

We know how important context is when interpreting anything, especially the Bible. Too often, beliefs are based on passages taken out of context, with disastrous results. Johnson refers us back to the context here. He says, "*...it must be considered so in the context of circumstances. The context is the overall work of Reconstruction from Ruin and the preparation of the Earth and a new world for Man. The term 'very good' does not mean 'perfect,' and the sea of separation placed between the world above and the world below was not good, but necessary. It would not be until the work of the Lord Jesus Christ on the cross that a way would be made for crossing that barrier (the sea, or waters, above the firmament).*

[65] http://www.kjvbible.org/firmament.html

[66] Ibid

"That particular "sea" is represented (in type) in a part of the design of Solomon's Temple known as the "Molten Sea." (See 1 Kings 7:23 and 2 Chronicles 4:2.) If you look at a diagram layout of the Temple you will see that this sea is between the Altar and the main part of the Temple where the Holy Place and Most Holy Place was.

"Here in the design of the Temple can be found in schematic form the structure of all things in type.

"The Altar where the sacrifices were offered represents where the Lamb of God was sacrificed. It represents the world that is below (the Earth & the first and second heavens).

"The Molten Sea is between those two lower heavens and the "Third Heaven" where the true Temple of God is located."[67]

I don't know about you, but when I read the words "Molten Sea" in the Scriptures, it is easy to wonder why God referred to the basin in this way. Numerous Bible scholars do not even mention it, except in some cases to imply that it is simply another name for the basin in which the priests washed.

The Molten Sea

Johnson continues with the subjects of the Third Heaven and the Molten Sea, looking to Paul's letter to the Corinthians. He says, "*This now gives us a better understanding of what the Apostle Paul was talking about in the book of II Corinthians 12:2, where he speaks of a place called the 'third heaven': 'I knew a man in Christ above fourteen years ago, (whether in the body, I cannot tell; or whether out of the body, I cannot tell: God knoweth;) such an one caught up to the third heaven.'* (II Cor. 12:2)

"Although the "third heaven" is not directly mentioned in the Genesis narrative, the established structure of all things is defined in Genesis 1

[67] http://www.kjvbible.org/firmament.html

and, when understood, allows us to comprehend exactly where and what Paul was talking about when he mentions the "third heaven" in his letter. It also gives the reader a better understanding of John's vision in Revelation 4. Again, when the Lord God divided the waters He created a boundary, which presently exists between the two lower heavens (which constitute the firmament) and the third heaven (where the throne of God is). That boundary is that 'Sea,' and again that 'sea' is above the two heavens of the firmament. It is also likened in places to crystal or smooth glass: 'And the likeness of the firmament upon the heads of the living creature was as the colour of the terrible crystal, stretched forth over their heads above.' (Ezekiel 1:22)"[68]

In reading through that passage, we note that the Sea is *like* smooth glass or crystal. That could mean that it is extremely calm, with no wind at all, or it could be, as Johnson believes, "*The reason it appears like a smooth, crystal surface is because it is frozen: 'The waters are hid as [with] a stone, and the face of the deep is frozen.'* (Job 38:30)"[69]

Johnson points to other Scriptures that tell us more about this Sea, "*And they saw the God of Israel: and there was under his feet as it were a paved work of a sapphire stone, and as it were the body of heaven in his clearness.*" (Exodus 24:10)

"It is also likened to glass: 'And I saw as it were a sea of glass mingled with fire: and them that had gotten the victory over the beast, and over his image, and over his mark, and over the number of his name, stand on the sea of glass, having the harps of God.' (Revelation 15:2)

"With this understanding of exactly what the Firmament is and the structure of all things that God made during the seven days, many

[68] http://www.kjvbible.org/firmament.html
[69] Ibid

things that were previously obscure suddenly take on real meaning and enrich the reader's understanding."[70]

At this point, Johnson has presented all of the information and now takes the time to sum everything up for us.

"In summary, here is the structure of the physical world, as it now exists from the face of the Earth upwards:

- *The lower sea of physical waters (our seas and oceans)*
- *The first heaven (the atmosphere)*
- *The second heaven (outer space)*
- *The sea above outer space and below the third heaven (a sea of separation)*
- *And above it all, there is the Third Heaven.*

"That Christ may dwell in your hearts by faith; that ye, being rooted and grounded in love, May be able to comprehend with all saints what [is] the breadth, and length, and depth, and height; And to know the love of Christ, which passeth knowledge, that ye might be filled with all the fulness of God.

"The structure of the heavens is a recurring theme throughout the Bible. It is reinforced (in typology) throughout the Bible. For example, it is likened to the floors of a building, which we call "stories," and sure enough, the same word is even used in the KJV Bible.

"1. To describe the design of the heavens: '[It is] he that buildeth his stories in the heaven, and hath founded his troop in the earth; he that calleth for the waters of the sea, and poureth them out upon the face of the earth: The LORD [is] his name.' (Amos 9:6)

"2. This pattern of three (3) levels is also found is some other important things in the Bible, an example being the description of the design of

[70] Ibid

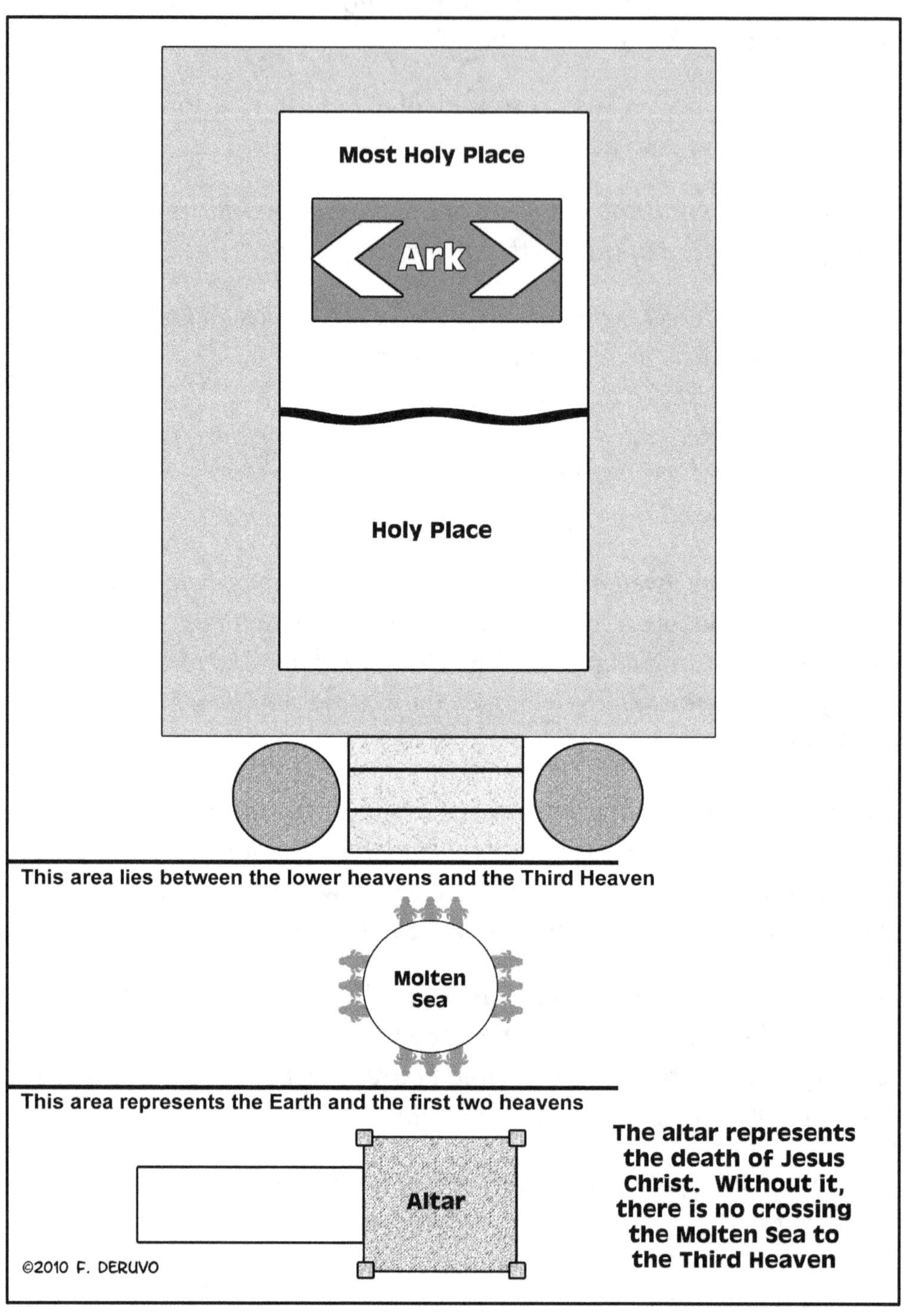
Most Holy Place
Ark
Holy Place
This area lies between the lower heavens and the Third Heaven
Molten Sea
This area represents the Earth and the first two heavens
Altar
The altar represents the death of Jesus Christ. Without it, there is no crossing the Molten Sea to the Third Heaven
©2010 F. DERUVO

Noah's Ark: 'A window shalt thou make to the ark, and in a cubit shalt thou finish it above; and the door of the ark shalt thou set in the side thereof; [with] lower, second, and third [stories] shalt thou make it.' (Genesis 6:16)

"3. To describe the construction of the Temple: 'The door posts, and the narrow windows, and the galleries round about on their three stories, over against the door, cieled with wood round about, and from the ground up to the windows, and the windows [were] covered;' (Ezekiel 41:16)

"In the construction of Moses' Tabernacle in the wilderness there were three main parts:

1) *The outer court, where the brazen altar of sacrifice was.*
2) *The Holy Place, where the candlestick, table of shewbread, and golden altar of incense were.*
3) *The Holy of Holies where the Ark of the covenant was. Also note that between parts two and three was a curtain for a partition, which matches the "sea" above the firmament (in type) in the structure of the Three Heavens. It is no coincidence that all these Biblical things have a similar three-tiered structure.*

"There is much spiritual insight to be gained in further study of those things:

- *Three Heavens*
- *Three levels inside Noah's Ark*
- *Three floors in a section of the Temple*
- *Three sections to Moses' Tabernacle*

"Concerning the design of the Temple, keep in mind that Moses' tent Tabernacle and Solomon's Temple both had three (3) main parts:

- *The outer court*

- *The holy place (where the table, lamp and incense alter was, outside the veil)*
- *The Most Holy Place (where the Ark was, behind the veil)*

"As you can see, this theme of structure based on threes is consistent throughout the Bible. Even the structure of the Earth has three (3) main divisions: the core, the mantle, and the crust.

"Does the Universe really have a structure? When you go into outer space is there really any such thing as up and down? Is there a top and bottom? Does the cosmos have a definite shape? We cannot observe such in our three-dimensional view of the universe.

"I found an interesting article in volume 25, number 1, of Discover Magazine (page 37) where this subject is briefly discussed. Using observations from the Wilkinson Microwave Anisotropy Probe, or WMAP, which observes the faint cosmic microwave background of space, scientists have been able to reconstruct the "exact proportions" of the cosmos. They found that there is only 4% "normal" matter, 23% "dark" matter and "73% "dark energy" out there. To quote the article: 'Those figures indicate that the universe is flat and will most likely continue to expand forever'.

"This is what can be observed, but is that all that is really out there? Not according to the Bible! In the words of Lord Himself there is a world above the one we live in and can observe: 'And he said unto them, Ye are from beneath; I am from above: ye are of this world; I am not of this world.' (John 8:23)

"Just because we cannot observe or understand something does not disprove its existence."[71]

In all their attempts to denigrate the Scriptures, and present their lies as truth, neither the Pleiadians nor any other group of entities

---

[71] http://www.kjvbible.org/firmament.html

ever spends this amount of time bringing the truth of Scripture to bear on itself.

When they are dealing with the average individual involved in the New Age movement, they do not need to be biblically specific. They can treat the Bible haphazardly, counting on the fact that the average person knows little to nothing about the Bible.

Though Lia Shapiro spent some time reading and studying the Bible, she never explains what her beliefs were during and after that time. Who knows how much sense it made to her?

Tickling the Ears of the Unchurched

This method is fine for the unchurched individual, approaching them with platitudes and sweeping generalizations. In such a case, the fact that these spiritual beings toss in a few direct references *to* the Bible and even opt to point to Jesus and events *from* the Bible is good enough to allow them to pass the test for the average New Ager. Because they have little to no background in Scripture, it is sufficient to merely tickle their ears with references to the Bible. The recipient of that information has no clue anyway, but since they sound authoritative and they are referencing something that authentic Christians deem to be fully authoritative, it passes the muster.

We could spend a good deal of time highlighting information from other books of the same genre as Shapiro's, books like *The Pleiadian Agenda*, by Barbara Hand Clow, or *The Pleiadian Workbook*, by Amorah Quan Yin. We could also delve into *The Aquarian Gospel of Jesus Christ*, by Levi. The result is the same though. The beliefs that god is within you exists in all these books. It is a process of finding your way within (going into "inner space"), until you are able to *unlock* that deity, which resides within you. Once that is accomplished, the world is your oyster and your realities are there for the making.

It seems good enough for Pleiadians and other beings to mention little regarding the Bible to New Agers and the rest of the unchurched population who yearn for something more from outer space. What about people who *attend* church who may have more than a passing knowledge of Scripture, and who may even firmly believe themselves to be Christian? What about those who are authentic Christians, yet have never bothered to take the time to study His Word so that they will become approved of God? For these individuals, something else entirely is needed. Like the Nephilim demons and fallen angels who provide what the proponents of New Age need to believe that these beings are altruistic in nature, there are other Nephilim demons and fallen angels to give the *churched* with some biblical knowledge what they need.

Chapter 11
Sympathy for the Devil

Within the visible Church, there are individuals that I believe are empowered by Satan to accomplish his ends (with God's permission). Satan uses these individuals through their intellect, their ability to write, and their ability to draw other people to them. Their main job, as I see it, is to do exactly what the Nephilim demons and fallen angels do as Pleiadians. That is, they are to confuse, and ultimately pull people away from the one, true God.

These people do this in any number of ways, but they mainly accomplish their goals through a series of questions, with implied answers. They also bring a bit of tongue-in-cheek flavor to their instruction. Because they are so intelligent, people find it difficult to disagree with them. Because people are hard pressed to offer rebuttals to what they hear, they are often dragged along at great peril.

I would like to be *emphatically* clear here. What I am *not* saying is that these individuals are permanently agents of Satan. It seems clear however, that to advance his goals, the enemy is certainly using them. Might they become authentically saved at some point in time, if they are not currently? I believe they could, though of course they would state that they *are* saved now. Like anything, the proof is in the pudding so to speak. It is understood in *what* they espouse, and *how* they espouse it.

In many ways, the battle lines have been drawn long ago, and they are simply coming more into focus as time moves along. People at the head of the Emergent Church movement have done a great deal of damage in the visible Church, as they have and continue to pull people away from the authentic gospel to an alternate one, which of course is no gospel at all.

Philosophical Meanderings

In the espousal of their philosophical meanderings, they have succeeded in often drawing large crowds of followers to them. Yet, these individuals when all is said and done offer nothing except *words* that are designed to make people feel good (all except authentic, spiritually mature Christians, that is).

People desperately want to feel good today. They want to believe that they are okay. They do not feel good or believe they are okay, and so they look outside of themselves for a savior, someone who can point the way. Because they are focused on how they *feel* within themselves, they want that uncertainty to be eradicated from within them.

What people like Brian McLaren, Philip Gulley, and others do is present another Jesus. They do it in a way that is often viewed as non-threatening to the uninitiated. This applies to professing Christians, as well as those who have some religious experience in their background, but have never taken the time to understand the claims of Jesus Christ.

As strongly as I believe the Nephilim demons and fallen angels work through the intricate system of lies and deceit created by their alter egos found in the Pleiadians, I believe these same beings or others in their ranks have spent centuries bringing humanity to the point where it is now fashionable not only to question the veracity of Scripture, but to routinely deny that veracity. The Pleiadians who deal with unchurched people for the most part can simply come right out and say that the Bible is wrong here and there, or mistranslated or they can say that Jesus was completely misunderstood by His contemporaries and certainly by modern civilizations.

However, *unlike* the Pleiadians who preach just about any gobbledygook they choose, which is *accepted*, spiritual entities who often speak through the works of people like McLaren, Gully, Warren, Foster and others who have become known as leaders within the Emergent Church must tread carefully because they are dealing with people who have at least *some* religious training. Because of that, their approach is carefully nuanced, so that it seems on the surface to pass the test. A look below the surface however reveals the true meaning and their true intent. They wish to deceive and do so by carefully crafted messages, which slowly draw their readers and listeners to them, like a spider carefully drawing the fly with the web she has created. Note also that many of these individuals are extremely intelligent, though not always. Their ability (as in the case of Brian McLaren) to present lies as truth is couched in verbiage that the average person finds difficult to disagree with and because of that, have little trouble adopting those beliefs.

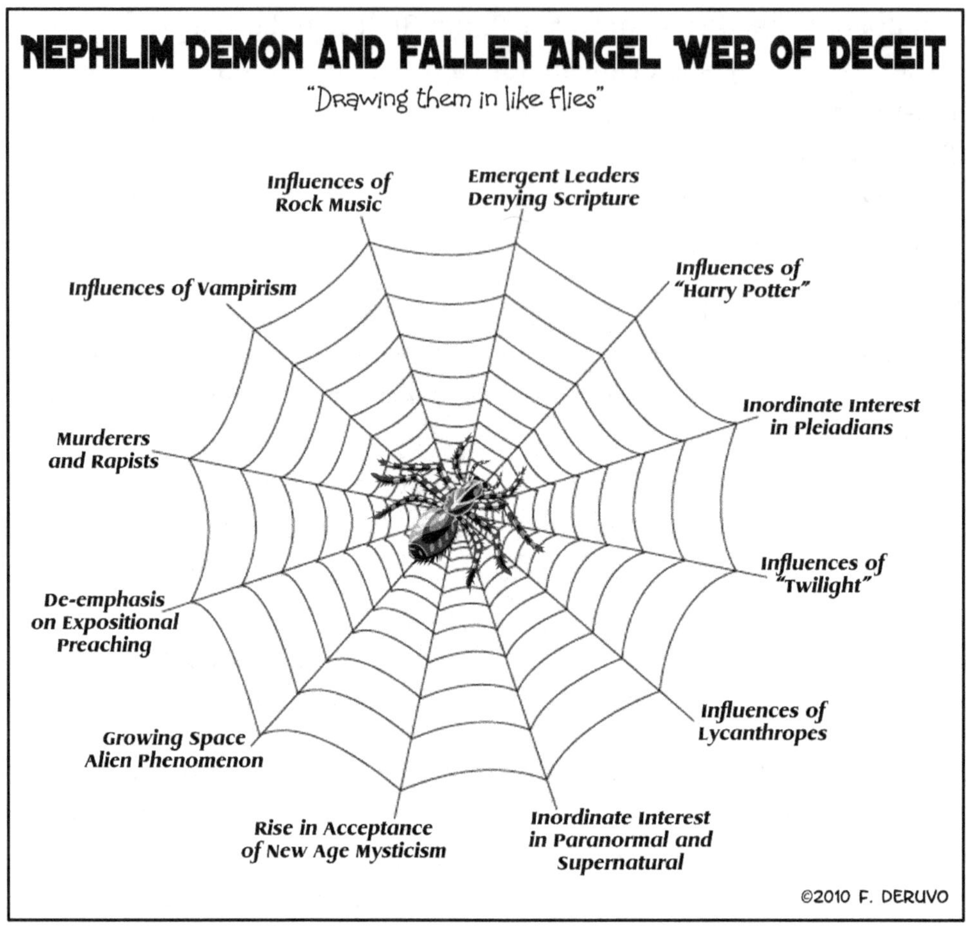

While the individual leaders within the Emergent Church would undoubtedly come right out and deny the veracity of Scripture, or the virgin birth, or the death of Christ by crucifixion, or that His death is substitutionary (if they thought they could get away with it), they cannot *immediately* do that. They must take the time to *build* their audience and then gently, over time, introduce more and more *error*.

If we stop to consider the fact that, the Nephilim demons and fallen angels have created a very intricate web of deceit, which touches on most areas within our society, we soon realize that their overall plan is extremely *intricate* leaving little to nothing up for grabs. Whether it is rock, or heavy metal music, or an inordinate fascination with vampirism, or werewolves, or the desire to be like Harry Potter, or a full frontal attack by the Gay community on the morals of God's Word, the meaning behind all of these things is clear. They are all designed to draw people in so that they will be deceived. Once they are deceived, they can be taught nearly anything without objection.

It really does not matter what avenue a Nephilim demon or fallen angel takes to ensnare a person, because they have provided something for everyone. They all lead to the same place, while at the same time their plans and paths consistently work to achieve a complete breakdown of society so that people will become more open to the change that is on its way. By looking at the web of deceit on the previous page, it should become clear that it really does not matter where a person's interest lies. They might be completely enamored with Harry Potter, vampires, and werewolves. They may also come to embrace the Twilight books and movies.

Because of the emphasis on the supernatural and paranormal in these movies and franchises, people who embrace these things, are much more likely to embrace *other* things connected to that web. With the exception of the "murderers and rapists," everything seems to blend, so why is that category there? As discussed previously, Nephilim are more than willing to create an avenue for everyone. At the same time, if they are able to inhabit or possess certain individuals that allow them (Nephilim) to do what they want for their physical enjoyment, the better.

In the end, everything on that web is meant to *hurt* humanity. It is meant to *destroy*, and destroy it will *if allowed*. The Nephilim do not really care how they capture the minds of human beings, so long as they *capture* them. Once they imprison the mind, they have the *will*. Once they have the will, they have *control*. That is in reality, what it amounts to in every sense. Each one of those headings on the web are ways that the Nephilim demons and fallen angels gain access to a person's heart and mind (will), and from there it is one step away to control. Since everyone has different personalities, likes and dislikes, it makes sense that many avenues would be needed.

The Nephilim demons, the fallen angels, along with Satan himself are more than willing to give humanity what they want, as long as they get what *they* want in return. I believe that books by people like Brian McLaren, Rick Warren, Richard Foster, Tony James, Philip Gulley, and many others go a long way in bridging the gap between the kingdom of darkness and this world.

Chapter 12

Liar

Both Brian McLaren and Philip Gulley have published books in which they not only question the orthodoxy of Christianity, but they deny some of the basic and accepted meanings of it, and make no apologies for doing so.

In any number of previously published books, McLaren has spent time chipping away at the meaning of the many of the sacred doctrines held dear by authentic Christians for generations. While he might be offended at this comment, it bears noting that he is working for someone, but that someone is *not* God.

McLaren is a great writer, very warm, sincere, and inviting. When his subject becomes too intense and serious, he is right there to interject a joke or quip. He tries not to personally attack Christianity, unfortunately, to those who *know* what Christianity stands for, it is clear that he does just that. He prefers instead to condemn what he sees as unloving attitudes within Christendom.

McLaren is obviously well versed and skilled in dialogue, at least in written form. The snippets of speeches he has given publicly present a soft-spoken and even mundane individual (at least this is my perception of him). McLaren's approach is mainly philosophical and this is exactly what he would like his readers to emulate. Philosophy winds up asking a good many questions, without necessarily being able to supply the answers. In fact, philosophy if rightly understood does not seek to define absolutes at all. It is the *process* of thinking and discussing that is the end result.

Philosophy is best understood in the actual *discussion*, not in any answers that may flow from that discussion. Philosophical thoughts and outlooks actually preempt declarative statements. They address issues by questioning those issues. What drives the issue? What does it really say? Why does it say what it says? Is there another way to understand what is being stated or asked?

Arguing with Satan is Futile

I cannot imagine holding my own with Satan in a discussion. It would be futile because his ability to discuss *and* convince far outweighs anything I might bring to the discussion. It is no wonder that Jesus never really got into arguments with Satan and that is not due to any suggestion that Christ would have *failed* in an argument with him. The point is that if Jesus did not bother arguing with Satan, then we should obviously not attempt to do it either.

When I read books by McLaren and others, the thought that immediately comes to mind is that I believe they are saying what

Satan would say. While I am certain they would find that statement offensive, the fact remains that this is what *comes to my mind*. I did *not* say that Satan *possesses* them (although that could be the case). I said I *believe* that what they are saying are things that *Satan* would *say*. Why? It is because at every turn, McLaren and others attempt to cast huge shadows of doubt on the truth of Scripture. These men do their level best (and granted, they do it well), to gently yet firmly lead their readership to a "new" and "different" understanding of the age-old truths upon which Christ founded His Church.

In his latest book *A New Kind of Christianity*, McLaren continues chiseling away at the solid foundation of the invisible Church by attempting wholeheartedly to *negate* the doctrine of salvation and the substitutionary death of Christ.

Overarching Story Line of the Bible

McLaren really wastes no time touting what I believe to be his heretical views of Scripture. In his chapter titled "*What is the Overarching Story Line of the Bible*," he questions a number of things, but he builds up to it, slowly, questioning the age-old belief that most people will wind up (unfortunately and tragically) in hell through their lack of belief. Because of this, McLaren asks, "*Can we dare to wonder, given an ending that has more evil and suffering than the beginning, if it would have been better for this story never to have begun?*"[72] The obvious *implied* answer is "*yes, it would have been better if this story had not been written, Mr. McLaren, because we have obviously misunderstood it so badly.*"

[72] Brian D. McLaren *A New Kind of Christianity* (New York: HarperCollins, 2010), 35

Undaunted that he has suggested that the Bible is essentially *manufactured* (or at least its meaning is), with the meaning up for grabs, McLaren continues, "*In recent years, hundreds of writers, pastors, and thinkers – probably thousands – have dared to tweak various elements or lines in this story, I among them. We might question conventional theories of atonement or the nature and population of hell or whether concepts like original sin or total depravity need to be modified. In other words, we suggest that this line should be a little longer, that one a little short. But seldom do we question whether this shape as a whole is morally believable and whether it can be found in the Bible itself. Did Abraham hold it, or Moses, or Jeremiah, or Jesus, Paul, or James? Is it ever explicitly taught in Scripture? Was it held in the first three centuries of Christian history? Does it help make sense of the Bible – revealing more than it conceals? Does it contribute to a higher vision of God, a deeper engagement with Christ, a more profound experience of the Holy Spirit? Does it motivate us to love God, neighbor, stranger, and enemy more wholeheartedly? It dawned on me only gradually that the answer to each of the above questions was no.*"[73]

I am frankly not sure where to begin with a rebuttal. First, the question must be asked in all seriousness, *which Bible is McLaren reading and which particular history books has he studied?* The plain fact of the matter is the *exact* opposite of the answer that McLaren arrived at from his musings. Rather than do their own research, people will simply take McLaren's word for it.

McLaren essentially presents the story of the Bible as six pieces, which all fit together quite nicely. According to McLaren, the Bible begins with *Eden*, quickly moves to *the Fall*, creating a world in *condemnation*, with the end result being a majority of people *being in hell*, while a minority of people *being in heaven* (cf. pages 33-35 of *A New Kind of Christianity*). Frankly, all McLaren does here is highlight

[73] Brian D. McLaren *A New Kind of Christianity* (New York: HarperCollins, 2010), 35

events or *aspects* of things biblical, but he also misses a tremendous amount. Of course, that does not bother him, because he is on a mission to re-visualize the Bible.

In reading a number of articles by Gaines Johnson, he states that the overarching theme of the Bible is *"the 'Kingdom' and who will rightfully rule it is the CENTRAL THEME of the Scripture and all history of the ages."* While McLaren provides us with "markers" in the biblical record, Johnson provides with a *real* overarching theme or story.[74]

W. Graham Scroggie believes the overall theme of the Bible is *The Unfolding Drama of Redemption*, which is the title of one of his most famous books. There, he draws the line of God's plan of redemption from Genesis to Revelation. McLaren sees no such theme apparently.

I may be spitballing here, but the truth is that Johnson's overarching or central theme to the Bible and all of history (along with Scroggie's) is far more accurate than McLaren's. In Johnson's view, we come to understand that the entirety of all that has happened and will happen connects with the question of who will be the ultimate ruler of God's kingdom, God or Satan. As stated, McLaren simply provides us with scenes from the play, but not the entire play itself.

Getting back to McLaren's questions in which he responded with an unequivocal 'no' to each, we can view them individually. Regarding Abraham, do we need to remind people that the Bible had not been written when Abraham walked this earth? As far as we know, Moses had written not one word of Scripture when Abraham lived, with the only possible exception being the book of Job. That book alone reveals to us a side of God that most prefer to reject. There we see a God that we might be tempted to think of in terms of a trickster or certainly someone who does not seem to care all that much because

[74] Gaines Johnson *The Pre-Adamite World and Origin of Satan* (www.kjvbible.org)

of all that He allowed Satan to inflict on Job. It is assumed then, that McLaren may not view the book of Job in a literal fashion, but merely a book that tells another "story;" a fable with a message.

What about Moses? Since McLaren seems to have a difficulty believing that the orthodox view of God, hell, and salvation should be questioned, one only wonders how McLaren can *possibly* state or imply that during Moses' time, there is *nothing* that occurred which provides greater insight into the nature and character of God, or that this understanding *fails* to help us make sense of the Bible, contributes to a higher vision of God, and more? I am at a loss.

Do not the trials, tribulations, and problems brought to bear on the Israelites (usually because of their failure to *believe* God and follow His commands from the heart), point to a God of unfathomable majesty, justice, patience, and love? McLaren likely sees this God as a monster though.

How is it possible to read nearly any portion of Jeremiah and come away with a *lower* view of God, or a view that sees God through a vision that is *less* than what one might expect from the only Omnipotent God?

Jesus spoke of hell *more* than He spoke of any other subject, so again, how does McLaren arrive at his viewpoint that the old "story" that we have all apparently bought into without full investigative queries, is a story that takes away from God, rather than adds to our understanding of His eternal character and nature?

According to McLaren, Paul had a particular *view* of Jesus, but in the end, it was simply Paul's view of Christ, as seen through the eyes of a dyed in the wool Pharisee, who came to know Christ on the road to Damascus.[75] McLaren's big problem is that we never allegedly see

---

[75] Brian D. McLaren *A New Kind of Christianity* (New York: HarperCollins, 2010), 36

the real Jesus, as He has been disseminated to us through others, like Paul, like Augustine, like Aquinas, etc.

McLaren believes we should not simply "***locate Jesus primarily in light of the story that has unfolded since his time on earth,*** *[because] we will understand him in one way. But* ***if we see him emerging from within a story that had been unfolding through his ancestors, and if we primarily locate him in that story, we might understand him in a different way.***"[76] McLaren believes the story that we have of Jesus today came about due to the Greek philosophy of the times, specifically directly from Plato, of all people. McLaren states without equivocation that "*nobody in the Hebrew Scriptures ever talked about original sin, total depravity, 'the Fall,' or eternal conscious torment in hell, a suspicion began to grow in me about where the six-lined narrative might possibly have come from.*"[77] This is where Plato appears, and he is the person to which McLaren refers.

Does anyone else see what McLaren has done though? In one swell swoop, he states that within the context and confines of the Hebrew Scriptures, no one discussed, or spoke of the doctrines of original sin, total depravity, or eternal hell. Again, I am left wondering *where* McLaren gets his information, because as far as I can tell, from reading through his book, while he *makes* these declarative statements, he does little to nothing to back them up with actual, uncompromising fact.

If we consider the Hebrew Scriptures from Genesis alone, it appears that not only does the text bear out the fact that Adam and Eve sinned (thus this was the original sin of mankind), but *RAMBAM* (R'Mose Ben Nachman) adds his own comments that clearly define

---

[76] Ibid, 36-37

[77] Ibid, 37

this act as a form of rebellion against God.[78] Beyond this, in the Hebraic-Roots Version of the Scriptures, it is also clear that the intended meaning of the passage where God confronts Adam and Eve after their sin, resulted in their expulsion from the Garden of Eden.[79]

Original Sin?

I suppose that McLaren believes that even *if* Adam and Eve sinned (which would obviously be classified as the "original sin" for all of humanity since Adam was the first human being on earth, from which all other human begins came to be), then that sin might not have necessarily been passed along to successive generations. The problem with this philosophical viewpoint is that one must ask, how is it possible that the results of their sin (which caused spiritual and eventual physical death), would *not* have passed along to every other individual who came from Adam's loins? Is this not what Paul essentially means in Romans 5:12. "*Wherefore, as by one man sin entered into the world, and death by sin; and so death passed upon all men, for that all have sinned,*" (KJV). Paul, reading the same narrative that McLaren reads, comes away from that narrative understanding that due to Adam and Eve's failure to continue to obey God, death was the result. That death – both spiritual and physical – could not avoid passing along to everyone else that came after Adam and Eve, unless they had come from a different lineage. This of course, was impossible since there were no others except Adam and Eve.

While McLaren is busy touting the alleged virtues and dominance that the Greco-Roman worldview had on the rest of the world, his implication is clear that the Bible's original meaning was literally transformed through the filtering process of Greek thought. He then claims in so many words, that we here in the United States, inherited this same slant because that is how it was passed down to us.

---

[78] The Torah with RAMBAM's Commentary (Translated, Annotated, and Elucidated – Artscroll, Mesorah Publications:2007),108, 123, 126

[79] Hebraic-Roots Version of the Scriptures (Institute for Scripture Research, 2005), 8

The fact that there are numerous denominations all with various viewpoints of the Bible, the fundamentals of the faith, and understanding of God must have slipped by McLaren completely. *"Every time we use terms like 'the Fall' and 'original sin,' I believe, many of us are unknowingly importing more or less of this package of Greco-Roman, non-Jewish, and therefore nonbiblical concepts like smugglers bringing foreign currency into the biblical economy or tourists introducing invasive species into the biblical ecosystem."*[80]

At least McLaren is clear in his meaning here, but it is also clear that in spite of his ability to define things in philosophical terms, his conclusions fly in the face of the facts of history. His conclusions also unintentionally wind up reducing God to a having a minor part in the creation and maintenance of His own Word. Unfortunately, McLaren simply continues on, unabated by his obvious lack of truthfulness, speaking like a politician who is running his re-election campaign.

Facts are No Friend of McLaren

Facts do not seem to bother McLaren and they certainly do not get in his way. Believing the current understanding of the Bible to be wrong, McLaren intones, "*more and more of us are defecting from the project of cosmetically enhancing this story and trying to rehabilitate the image of Theos. We want to try reading the Bible frontward for a while, to let it be a Jewish story that, through Jesus, opens to include all humanity. We believe it is time to firmly escort the Greco-Roman reframing of the biblical narrative to the door and seek what master songwriter Michael Kelly Blanchard calls 'the other God' – the God of Abraham, Isaac, and Jacob, not the god of the Greek philosophers and Roman potentates."*[81] Isn't that wonderful? Don't you just feel that McLaren is finally going to take us all from the path of "error," to place us firmly on the path of "truth"? Apparently, up to this point in time, God has been unable to do that through anyone else.

---

[80] Brian D. McLaren *A New Kind of Christianity* (New York: HarperCollins, 2010), 43

[81] Brian D. McLaren *A New Kind of Christianity* (New York: HarperCollins, 2010), 45

Of course, McLaren's next chapter – *Setting the Stage for the Biblical Narrative* – is his attempt to rewrite the Bible's account with the "true" meaning, which he believes the Greco-Roman view tainted miserably. Of course, it is not long before McLaren tries his hand at Eschatology, using Micah 4:2-4, Isaiah 2:4; 11:6-9; 65:17-25, Joel 2:27-29 and Hosea 2:18-19 as his jumping off point. *"Many of us modern Christians, having been trained to read the Bible within the six-line Greco-Roman narrative, 'know' what to do with these passages. We push them to the distant future, beyond history as we know it, applying them either to heaven, a literalist 'millennial' period, or a little bit of both. But what if we were to receive these images in a different way?"*[82]

McLaren's method is to place us all in the book of Genesis, during that period, and combine that with the Exodus narrative of what he calls *"liberation and formation."*[83] He then clarifies his meaning by asking, *"what if we were to receive these images as a vision of the kind of future toward which God is inviting us in history? What if we saw them as less as an eternal destination* beyond *history and more as a guiding star* within *it, less as a literal description and prediction and more as a poetic promise and hope, less as a doctrine to be debated and more as an unquenchable dream that inspires us to unceasing constructive action? What if we saw them as a good future unfolding in time, not a perfect state beyond time?"*[84]

As Marty might say in *"Back to the Future,"* that is *heavy*, isn't it? In reality though, all McLaren is truly saying is that the gospel of Jesus Christ should be seen in terms of what the Christian *can do* to *improve* society, *externally*, whereas the actual gospel does not improve man, but actually gives him a brand new spirit, making him a totally new creation!

---

[82] Ibid, 62
[83] Ibid, 62
[84] Ibid, 62

It's All in the Allegorizing

The reality of course, is that McLaren is doing nothing more and nothing less than viewing Scripture *allegorically.* Viewing Scripture allegorically allows and even encourages the interpreter to read into the text any meaning that is convenient for him. Whether he believes he is the first one to do that is another thing, but the truth remains that when people opt to read *into* (and that is exactly what he is doing though he would deny it), the text of Scripture, just about any meaning can be derived from it.

In the normal mode of interpretation, most biblical scholars agree that the Bible should be understood in the *context* in which it was written. Moreover, the actual languages – Hebrew, Greek, and Aramaic – should be studied to determine actual meaning from definition. Of course, final meaning cannot be determined apart from *context of the verbiage.* The history, grammar, context, and culture should be understood before attempting to interpret Scripture. Mr. McLaren does none of that, preferring instead to skip through the Scriptures, defining meaning based on *his preconceived paradigm*, while wailing that those of us who follow the *normally accepted* rules of interpretation (for any book of antiquity) are the real problem, because we supposedly force our preconceived ideas onto the sacred text.

It is also very clear that for McLaren, the Bible is not *sacred.* It seems clear enough that he does not view it as having been written ultimately *by God*, with God Himself indicating that His Word (written or spoken) is the final authority. This is exactly why McLaren can denounce those of us who believe that homosexuality as well as same-sex marriage is wrong. However, it is clear enough from the writings of Moses that homosexuality was a terrible sin in God's eyes (cf. Leviticus 18:22; 20:13). Of course, McLaren would rebut with ceremonial and non-moral issues such as, *should women be allowed to wear pants (men's clothing) today since it was against the Law in Moses' day?* What people like McLaren consistently *fail* to grasp is that there is a difference between *ceremonial* law, *moral* law and *incidental* laws.

All Christians are to obey the *moral* Law of God. That has never changed. McLaren and others routinely get around this by touting Jesus as a *loving* person. This of course, presupposes that those of us who state that homosexuality is *wrong* are not simply stating a fact, as far as God is concerned, but are actually making those statements out of *hatred*.

Returning to McLaren's belief that the previous passages cited from Isaiah, Joel, Hosea, and Micah should be viewed from *his* perspective, we come to a conflict. When McLaren does this, he immediately states that *prophetic* passages of Scripture are not prophetic at all, but have been *deemed* prophetic by those who came after the texts were written. This view though, does not square with Judaism at all. Orthodox Jews (who do not consider Jesus, or Paul, or James or anyone outside of the Torah and Tanakh unless it is their own sages and Jewish rabbis), understand that there are *many* areas of Scripture that are purely *prophetic*, pointing to a specific time in *their* future. They believe many have not been fulfilled at all...yet. Obviously, they continue to look for their Messiah, based on numerous Old Testament prophecies.

Many passages *have* been fulfilled in Jesus Christ alone. It would seem that since these passages – first penned *long* before Jesus Christ ever walked this earth as a Man in and around Jerusalem – were *fulfilled* literally by this same Jesus, does it not stand to reason that the Bible is filled with *prophetic* discourse?

McLaren prefers to believe that it is *not*. Certainly, that is his prerogative, but to foist his *uneducated* opinion couched in intelligent sounding verbiage, on the masses is something that he should be extremely careful about doing. I find it remarkable for instance, that some critics castigate the book of Daniel. They firmly believe that it was not written by *the* Daniel of that time, but by an imposter who came long after that original Daniel had lived and died.

This imposter – they believe – actually looked *backwards* and recorded the events *as if* they had not yet taken place. Why do the critics put forth this argument? They view the book with a jaundiced eye because the *accuracy* of the book of Daniel is *uncanny*. Never in a million years would they venture to think, believe, or admit that the book of Daniel could be fully straightforward. Instead, they prefer to relegate it to the work of an imposter who did nothing more than record history by looking backwards, as if it had not yet occurred.

I cannot help but wonder why McLaren even wasted the time going *back* to those Old Testament passages? Why did he not simply refer to Jesus? What, has he gotten tired of twisting Jesus' words into something they are not (i.e. a *social* gospel)? Apparently, he now believes he needs to go back to the "beginning" to prove to us that this same social gospel message was there all the time, hidden in the text. We have simply been unable to see it due to our proclivities to see the Bible through the Greco-Roman filter. However, *Super-McLaren* has come to our rescue, unmasking the concealed truth, which has remained hidden for roughly 4,000 years.

McLaren comments on what he believes is his own wisdom. *"If we take this third narrative in this way, we are immediately freed from arguments about a deterministic future...because the future in this approach is waiting to be created; it is not fatalistically predetermined. God hasn't already prerecorded history so that it waits like digital information on a disk, already 'made' but only being 'played' in real time. No, by taking this new approach, the narrative of the peaceable kingdom becomes the desired future toward which the people of God orient themselves, the constellation they set course and sail by, the dream or goal or vision or imagination they pursue. In this view, history and life are not prerecorded: life is 'live.' History isn't a 'show' –*

not even a 'reality show.' History is unscripted, unrehearsed reality, happening now - really happening. (You might want to pinch yourself before reading on, and ask yourself if you really believe the previous sentence.)"[85]

Moving On

Okay, I pinched myself, but only because I was trying to determine whether or not what I had just read was presented by someone who deems themselves to be *intelligent*. Look, what McLaren is doing here is absolutely *nothing* new at all. In fact, if people are not attacking the doctrine of the deity of Christ, or the Trinity, one of the first things they manage to go after is Eschatology. McLaren is merely couching his terms in quaint vignettes, presented to us as a football coach would give in his before game speech. In both cases, the attempt is to get the team pumped up. McLaren is busy trying to free people from what he would likely call the tyranny of orthodoxy (hey, great title for his *next* book!), and he does it by *taking away* from God's sovereignty and *making us believe* that the future is ours to *control*. This is no different from what the New Age movement's leaders teach to their followers and adherents.

How is this any different from what Satan said to Eve in the Garden of Eden ("you shall be gods")? Isn't this it in a nutshell? It is the same *line*, and the same *lie*. You can control your own destiny. God is not in charge - *you are* and you need to get busy!

John Lanagan recently reviewed this same book for Lighthouse Trails, which appeared in a recent newsletter they sent out via email. In it, he refers to McLaren's Reformation (moving from Greco-Roman thought to a new paradigm), and asks, "*But does McLaren's paradigm vision really echo the Great Reformation? From the Reformation came the freedom of Sola Scriptura—the Word of God alone. The chains of a false religion were cast off. From the Reformation came men and*

[85] Brian D. McLaren *A New Kind of Christianity* (New York: HarperCollins, 2010), 62-63

women who were willing to die for the right to believe and proclaim Truth."[86]

This is exactly what McLaren *omits*. He does *not* believe that as the Bible came down through the ages, God had any kind of control over it at all. It was in the hands of men, and those men were not error-free. Therefore, their own slants came to bear on the text of Scripture, forever masking God's intended meaning. Never fear however, because McLaren (and a few others), are *finally* here to extricate the hidden meaning from its Greco-Roman prison.

Ultimately, McLaren's book contradicts Scripture at every point. He denies the substitutionary atonement, and original sin. He also denies that homosexuality is something that people should be calling *sin*. In fact, as Lanagan points out, "*when it comes to homosexuality, a good Christian is a silent Christian.*"[87] The fact that McLaren refers to himself as a Christian is beyond the pale, yet he does in a very matter of fact way. The sadder truth is that Brian McLaren has a B.A. in English, and as far as any theological training, he has *none*. However, he *was* awarded an *honorary* Doctorate of Divinity from Carey Theological Seminary in Canada, and is the founding pastor of Cedar Ridge Community Church (1986).[88]

I marvel at books from people like McLaren because he is very smooth. He tends to castigate those with whom he does not agree, but he does it with a smile on his face and a twinkle in his eye. McLaren is very *deceptive* and his deceptive nature continues to fool millions.

Enter Philip Gulley

Turning (ever so briefly) to another book by a completely different author, Philip Gulley, we learn that the Church is arguably *not*

---

[86] www.lighthousetrails.com
[87] Ibid
[88] http://en.wikipedia.org/wiki/Brian_McLaren

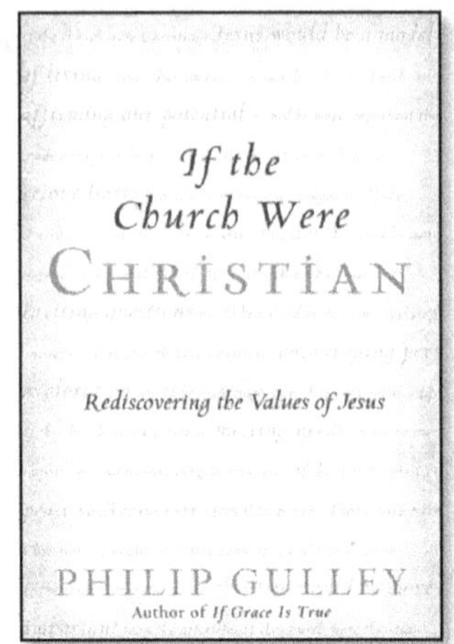

Christian. In fact, the title of his book is *If the Church Were Christian…* and it is also the title of his first chapter. The subtitle for that chapter is *Jesus Would Be a Model for Living Rather Than an Object of Worship.*

Philip Gulley, like McLaren, has an air of playfulness, serenity, and sincerity to him, which comes through in his book as well as the podcasts on his website. He seems approachable and filled with caring for the average individual. A Quaker minister, he came from a family with a Baptist father and Roman Catholic mother.

As he grew up, he learned of doctrines related to Jesus and the Bible. He learned that Jesus was born of a virgin. He learned that Jesus performed miracles, and he learned that Jesus was sinless. Of course, questions began to form in his mind, which led him to his own research where he soon learned that apparently, Jesus was *not* the only individual allegedly born of a virgin.

Gulley also realized that Jesus was not the only biblical character to perform miracles, as many before Him had done the same. Though at one time, Gulley fully believed that these stories of miracles were actually that, literal miracles performed by Jesus, he came to believe that these miracles were simply *attributed* to Him (without Him actually having done any) by people who deeply loved Him.

Gulley of course, also tackles the question of whether or not Jesus was sinless. He states, "*the classic definition of sin is to knowingly and willfully choose to do evil. Central to that understanding is one's mental, spiritual, and emotional capacity to make appropriate moral decisions.*"[89] Gulley then relates, "*Were I to learn that at the age of*

[89] Philip Gulley *If the Church Were Christian* (HarperCollins: 2010), 15

fifteen Jesus willfully disobeyed his parents or experienced adolescent feelings of sexual longing, my respect for his life and witness would not be diminished."[90]

The problem though is that Gulley's definition of sin is *not* a biblical definition of sin. John tells us that sin is *lawlessness* in 1 John 3:4. That is an excellent definition. It is man rebelling against God's authority, and deciding to live a life that is *against* God's moral Law. However, one would like to circumvent that by stating that it is a willful choice a person makes, the fact remains that God sees sin as something that is deep within our *nature*. That nature results in incidents of sin, all stemming directly from a corrupt or sinful nature that resides within each person.

Gulley also makes a statement that I first heard while writing my book *The Anti-Supernatural Bias of Ex-Christians*. Like one of the individuals I had based some of my research on, Gulley also states that he "*became enamored with the* ***life story of Jesus***."[91] (emphasis added)

Gulley's Experiences as Pastor

Gulley relates numerous incidents that he says occurred during his tenure as pastor. The thing that amazes is his spin on things. How do we know for instance that people actually responded as they did to his queries, as written in his book?

One situation involved a couple who was seeking divorce. He relates that "*In a perfect world, they would never have married individuals whose goals were incompatible with their own, but attraction, sexuality, and our need for partnership are powerful forces and not always receptive to reason. Fortunately, they were parting amiably, and were curious to know if I might be willing to conduct a ceremony that would dissolve their marriage while affirming their continued*

---

[90] Ibid, 15

[91] Philip Gulley *If the Church Were Christian* (HarperCollins: 2010), 17

friendship."[92] Obviously, Gulley assumes that this is the case. The reality though is that whether their goals matched or not, the truth of the matter is that they made a pledge to God and decided it was not worth keeping later on in life. Neither one was apparently willing to give up their own selfish goals to salvage their marriage.

Gulley relates how he had never heard of a ceremony, which would celebrate their amicable separation. Initially he says that he *"considered a ritual affirming divorce to be an inappropriate activity for the church."*[93] He asked the couple to allow him time to reflect on the idea. Gulley states that he wound up not doing it simply because the couple went ahead with the divorce and moved on, though not so amicably.

Interestingly, later on he was speaking to one of the church elders about this situation relating that maybe it was a good idea for the church to offer something like that. According to Gulley, *"Her response was swift and strong. 'That's precisely what is wrong with the church today. It doesn't stand for anything. Anything goes. We've got no business celebrating sin'."*[94]

Philip Gulley's book is 197 pages long. During the course of his book, he quotes a grand total of 14 Scripture references. That's it, just fourteen. McLaren actually does better, though it is interesting to see his spin on Scripture. Being an allegorist seems to know no boundaries at all.

Getting back to Gulley, while he refers to fourteen individual sections of Scripture, I could not help but notice that he also favorably quotes Eckhart Tolle and Joseph Campbell, both religious *mystics* though too often presented as "Christians." In quoting Tolle, Gulley states, *"In this book* A New Earth, *spiritual teacher Eckhart Tolle writes, 'Life isn't*

---

[92] Ibid, 58

[93] Philip Gulley *If the Church Were Christian* (HarperCollins: 2010), 58

[94] Ibid, 59

as serious as my mind makes it out to be.' When I first read those words, I felt an exhilarating sense of freedom and a keen awareness that life was to be appreciated and enjoyed. In sharp contrast, the church, which has always taken itself too seriously, has made us feel like our lives are in the balance, that we teeter on a precipice, our eternal well-being hanging on one decision, which must be made now, this moment, without delay. (The church will finally be faithful to Jesus when we feel the same urgency when faced with issues of justice and need.) The fears that escalate such gravity and gloom permeate the church, inhibiting our ability to live graciously and spontaneously."[95]

Eternity is Only Part of the Discourse

Let me see if I can summarize that. Gulley is saying that eternity should *not* be our biggest concern, and he has learned this "truth" from someone who is a "spiritual teacher." Then, he makes the disparaging remark that implies the church has done nothing with respect to social issues and justice. I have to wonder where this person has been living since his birth.

Is Philip Gulley *earnestly* attempting to say that the church has had *absolutely no* impact on the world through missions? Does he honestly believe that there are virtually no (or precious few) organizations that are working on these issues around the globe?

In a number of places, Gulley admits to being a Universalist[96] which is the belief that eventually, everyone *will* be saved. It is *because* of this errant belief that Gulley can take the position that the church needs to focus more on social issues and justice, rather than the eternal place where everyone will be – either heaven or hell.

I find it unconscionable frankly, that Gulley paints such a brutal picture of "fundamentalists" in his book. Apparently, we are routinely *bitter, angry, uncharitable, unwilling to forgive* and more.

---

[95] Philip Gulley *If the Church Were Christian* (HarperCollins: 2010), 83

[96] Ibid, 83

All of this certainly works to gain fans of his work, but how true are his characterizations? While I am not an idiot, and I fully realize that people *like the ones* Gulley describes do exist in nearly every church setting, my experience has enabled me to see that these people by far, are in the minority.

Gully asks on page 94, "*What would it mean if the church valued questions as much as answers?*" The implication of course, is that no questions are really allowed in church, certainly not the kinds of questions that cast a shadow over the fundamentals of the faith.

It continues to puzzle me why Gulley makes some of the points he makes. In his book, he relates how he learned that "*mountaintops were considered places of divine revelation and that Matthew used that setting to portray Jesus as a new lawgiver, a new Moses.*"[97] At the end of this sentence, he places a superscript number four (4) as a reference to an endnote. Reading the endnote states, "*Interestingly, Luke collected many of the same teachings but changed the setting to 'a level place.' Were I a fundamentalist, I would be troubled by this incongruity.*"[98]

Gulley's use of the term *incongruity* is his way of accusing the Bible of having a *contradiction* in it. This is sad, because what his comment *actually* says is that *he* understands little to nothing about the *setting* of the Sermon on the Mount (as recorded in Matthew and Luke).

Concisely, "a level place," as used by Luke simply means "*a piece of high tableland, by which they understand the same thing, as 'on the mountain,' where our Lord delivered the sermon recorded by Matthew (Mt 5:1).*"[99]

---

[97] Philip Gulley *If the Church Were Christian* (HarperCollins: 2010), 116

[98] Ibid, 119

[99] http://jfb.biblecommenter.com/luke/6.htm

William Hendricksen states, *"together with this intimate band of followers the Master 'went down' until he stood on 'a level place.' This may well have been a large level tract that coincides with the far larger gentle, grassy slope west of Tabgha, not far from Capernaum."*[100]

Walter L. Liefeld tells us, *"The 'level place (epi topou pedinou, v. 17) is apparently an area on the 'mountainside mentioned in Matthew 5:1. If it were a plain, such as Jesus often used for his teaching near the sea, just the words epi pedinou would probably have been used (Godet, p. 295)."*[101]

Even if this was *not* the case, does Gulley honestly believe that mountains do not have *flat areas* on them? Mt. Sinai has such areas near its peak, as do many mountains. What I find incongruous is Gulley's lack of ability (or willingness) to research the subject, but prefers instead to simply let it lie there concluding that it must be one of those contradictions that everyone says exists in the Bible. Because of that, the Bible cannot be trusted to be authoritative.

Gulley also quotes from Will D. Campbell, someone Gulley states was a *"Southern Baptist preacher and prophet…"*[102] In a footnote about Joseph Campbell, Gulley states, *"Joseph Campbell, now deceased, was a mythologist who specialized in the field of comparative religion. He came to my attention after viewing a PBS show by Bill Moyers called 'Joseph Campbell and the Power of Myth'."*[103]

I remember that program as well and two things struck me about it:

1. *Moyers – a seminary graduate seemed to hang on every word Campbell uttered, and*
2. *Campbell seemed to be impressed with every word he uttered*

---

[100] William Hendricksen *New Testament Commentary Luke* (Baker: 1978), 334
[101] Walter L. Liefeld *Expositor's Bible Commenatary – Matthew, Mark, Luke* (Zondervan: 1984), 890
[102] Philip Gulley *If the Church Were Christian* (HarperCollins: 2010), 123
[103] Ibid, 155

In the end though, Campbell's *Power of Myth* is nothing more and nothing less than New Age gobbledygook. I call it that, not because I do not understand it, but because *I do* understand it and what Campbell taught is nothing new. Like McLaren and Gulley, Campbell simply explained it in a different way, using different verbiage.

Grace?

At the back of Gulley's book, the publisher included an excerpt from another of Gulley's book *If Grace Is True*, co-written with James Mulholland. Because of that, it is difficult to know who is saying what, so it is probably best to understand that they are *both* saying and believing what they wrote in this book, interchangeably. The statement is made, "*I grew up believing we were destined for either heaven or hell. I was taught that only those who confessed their sins and accepted Jesus as their Savior before they died would live with God forever. All the rest would suffer hell's eternal torment. As a child, I'd never questioned this formula. It was simple and clear. As an adult, I'd held on to this belief despite life's complexities.*"[104]

I am not sure what "*life's complexities*" have to do with anything. In fact, the only way that I can understand where Gulley comes up with most of the beliefs that he has come up with, is in his *head*. Gulley, like any New Ager, is carried along by *feelings* of *peace, joy*, and *love*. This is what the New Ager chases and they will take any path to get there, except orthodox Christianity. Gulley seems to have arrived at his opinions without the aid of God's Word.

What it all boils down to for Philip Gulley (and we can assume James Mulholland), is something that he says lit his life on fire. "*Now I have a new formula. It too is simple and clear. It is the most compelling truth I've ever known. It is changing my life. It is changing how I talk about God. It is changing how I think about myself. It is changing how I treat other people. It brings me untold joy, peace, and hope. This*

[104] Philip Gulley *If the Church Were Christian* (HarperCollins: 2010), 202-203

truth is the best news I've ever heard, ever believed, ever shared. (Wait for it...-ed.) ***"I believe God will save every person.***"[105] (emphasis added) That is nice and I wish it were true. It is certainly a worthwhile thought, yet it goes against everything Jesus taught. As I stated earlier, Jesus spoke about hell more than any other subject. He came to *offer* salvation, but He never said that *everyone* would have it. In fact, He clearly referenced the fact that *few would find it* (comparatively speaking), (cf. Matthew 7:13).

The tragedy here is that from what I have gathered in reading Gulley's book, his theology is built *not* on the Bible, but on how he *feels* about issues and situations. Gully consistently points out what he believes are the flaws of the visible Church, yet offers precious little as any type of anecdote, based on Scripture.

Gulley, like McLaren, constantly vilifies those who deign to take God at His Word. Those of us who believe that people *will* be in hell, are seen as nutcases, Pharisees, or hatemongers. People like Gulley are loved by the world because he offers them nothing but *platitudes*; things that their itching ears love to hear. Platitudes however, do not save people. What platitudes wind up doing is creating a sense of being right, and then being comfortable with that, but they have no power to change.

Gulley says that because of the "truth" that everyone will be saved (and apparently, he does not realize that he has called God a liar), he is now treating others differently. Of course he is and for good reason! It is *easy* to treat people wonderfully if you think that they are all going to heaven, with no concern for their eternal soul!

It is just too bad that Jesus Himself never had this truth revealed to Him. If He had, He would have undoubtedly been far less judgmental where the Pharisees were concerned. I mean, they were *all* going to

---

[105] Ibid, 208-209

heaven anyway, so what was Jesus getting so upset about with them? Why didn't He just "chill out" and let things go? Instead, He often went head to head with the Pharisees, and other religious leaders, pointing out this flaw or that one. He certainly was argumentative, when according to Gulley, He obviously did not have to be.

Has Gulley Ever Cracked Open the Bible? I'm Just Saying...
Gulley may not be aware of these portions of Scripture that actually show Jesus castigating someone because of the fact that they had no truth, and they were keeping others from it as well. Salvation is and remains an extremely important aspect of everything that Jesus did for humanity. However, unbelievably, it is *not* the most important thing that He did. That may sound strange to some, but the clear reality is that *everything* that God has done and will do, is ultimately for one purpose. That purpose is to glorify Himself.

Gulley's theology (if you can call it that), fails on every level. At one point he states, "***The Christian gospel ought not to be that Jesus was God and we can find life in his death****. Our good news is that* ***we can find life in his example*** *– accepting the excluded, healing the sick, strengthening the weak, loving the despised, and challenging the powerful to use their influence redemptively.*"[106] (emphasis added)

Comments like these are overtly anti-God and therefore satanic. They are literally *doctrines of demons.* If all we get out of Jesus' life is that we should *imitate* Him, then there was absolutely *no purpose* in His death or resurrection. None whatsoever. Even faced with that very question in the excerpt from his *If Grace Is True*, he admits he has no answer, yet that fact has not diminished his resolve that God *will* save everyone. He believes he *will* have an answer one day.

It is also no surprise that Gulley denies the actuality of Adam and Eve, Noah, the Virgin Birth, the doctrine of the Trinity, and others,

[106] Philip Gulley *If the Church Were Christian* (HarperCollins: 2010), 26

referring to these things as *myths*. This is the result of choosing your own definitions and being your own final authority. This is the New Age and it *is* in the visible Church, regardless what some individuals prefer to believe.

People like McLaren, Gulley, Slabaugh, and others are happy to foist their erroneous doctrines and beliefs on the visible Church. They do so, because they long ago, decided that truth is *relative*. This is exactly what Satan *wants* us to believe. Oh wait he is just another myth.

Chapter 13

Turn, Turn, Turn

It would be easy to go on and on regarding this subject of the Nephilim demons and their cohorts, the fallen angels. However, the message of this book should be clear by now.

These malevolent, spiritual beings, under the guidance and sovereignty of their lord and master, Satan (who *remains* under God's sovereignty), have not only infiltrated every avenue of society, but have done so *gradually*, yet *consistently* over the centuries and especially within the past four to six decades. While they are busy using some individuals to create fear within society through their unprecedented and malicious crimes, other people have been used by Nephilim pretending to be aliens from space. They come to relay messages of hope and love, from allegedly benevolent beings from outer space. Still other people have been used in the *rock music* industry and the *television* and *movie* business to further warp an already warped society.

Nero's Ploy

The final segment of deceit – the New Age movement – has infiltrated the visible Church, with men and women plying their trade of lies by wrapping them in the swaddling clothes of palatable deceit. While people like McLaren and Gulley worry that the *evangelical church* has made its presence known in society, they are busy portraying evangelicals as modern day Pharisees, caring only for their own opinions, and willfully ignoring the plight of the downtrodden and less fortunate in society. It must be wonderful to have a scapegoat for all the ills in society. Nero used the same ploy, literally lighting up authentic Christians as torches to light his garden. I can only wonder if Gulley's "God will save everyone" belief would have been enough to get him through those difficult times.

The truth of the matter is that all of these things work together to push society toward its final preordained climax – a one-world government, with a one-world religion, overseen by a one-world ruler. The particular man of whom we speak, will exalt himself over everything and everyone and even blaspheme the holy Name of the Lord Most High, and will fancy himself a *god*. When he proclaims himself as god, the rest of the world will agree, because they have been taught for decades that *all are god already*. This man – the Antichrist – will muster his troops and the power of Satan will be his, for a time. Unfortunately, for him, his end is as sure as his father's (Satan), and it will come quickly once it comes.

What of you? Are you ready to meet your Creator? Your death could come at any time, any day, any hour, and any minute. Are you ready for what lies beyond this life? I certainly hope that this is the case. If not, why would you take any chances with the spiritual welfare of the only life you have? If you have not done so, I plead with you to acknowledge that Jesus is God, that He came as a Man (while still remaining God), lived a sinless life, died on Calvary's cross with the shedding of His blood, and rose again. He did this for you and for me.

Once you die, your chances are *gone*. You must understand that His life was given so that YOU might have LIFE. What does it take? You must believe with all your heart that Jesus is who He said He is, did what the Bible says He did and died a substitutionary death in your place and my place. Without His death, neither you nor I would have any chance of salvation. This is how deep and rich His love is, that He was willing to die a brutally painful death so that God's wrath could be poured out on Him...*instead of on you and me*.

Becoming a Christian is not defined by "believing" the story of the Bible or of Jesus. It is also not attempting to *imitate* Jesus with respect to eliminating social problems and injustices. Salvation is far more than that, and in fact, I believe that it is only through authentic salvation that an individual can do things in His strength that will stand for all of eternity. The rest of it is just me, myself, and I on the throne, regardless of how it may look to others, or even to me.

Becoming an authentic Christian is believing *in* Jesus and His atonement. It is *not* easy believism either. The Bible says that without *faith*, it is impossible to please God (Romans 3:23). Do you have the faith of the thief on the cross (cf. Luke 23)? Do you believe that He died for you? You can follow Gulley's and McLaren's beliefs and see where that takes you. I would prefer that you did not.

Do you want eternal life, or eternal death? The choice is yours. Make the right choice. Make it *now*.

Resources for Your Library

BOOKS:

- Agape Leadership (R. C. Chapman), by Peterson & Strauch
- Alien Encounters, by Chuck Missler
- The Alien Interviews, by L. A. Marzulli
- The Anti-Supernatural Bias of "Ex-Christians," by Fred DeRuvo
- The Church in Prophecy, by John F. Walvoord
- Confrontations, by Jacques Vallee
- Dictionary of Premillennial Theology, Mal Couch, Editor
- Dispensationalism Tomorrow & Beyond, by Christopher Cone, Ed.
- Earth's Earliest Ages, by G. H. Pember
- Exploring the Future, by John Phillips
- Fallen Angels, the Watchers and the Origins of Evil - Lumpkin
- Footsteps of the Messiah, by Arnold G. Fruchtenbaum
- Future Israel (Why Christian Anti-Judaism Must Be Challenged), by E. Ray Clendenen, Ed.
- Giants on the Earth, by Timothy Green Beckley
- Israelology, by Arnold G. Fruchtenbaum
- The Lost Book of Enoch, Transliteration by Joseph B. Lumpkin
- The Moody Handbook of Theology, by Paul Enns
- The Mountains of Israel, by Norma Archbold
- The Nephilim, by Patrick Heron
- Nephilim Stargates, by Thomas R. Horn
- The Pre-Wrath Rapture Answered, by Lee W. Brainard
- Pursuit of Holiness, by Jerry Bridges
- Things to Come, by J. Dwight Pentecost
- UFO End-Time Delusion, by David A. Lewis & Robert Shreckwise
- What on Earth is God Doing? By Renald Showers

Resources for Your Library (cont'd)

INTERNET:

- Anti-Preterist Blog — antipreterist.wordpress.com
- Ariel Ministries — www.ariel.org
- Berean Watchmen — www.bereanwatchmen.com
- Foothill Bible Church — www.foothill-bible.org
- Friends of Israel — www.foi.org
- Grace to You — www.gty.org
- Prophezine — www.prophezine.com
- Prophecy in the News — www.prophecyinthenews.com
- Study-Grow-Know — www.studygrowknow.com
- Study-Grow-Know Blog — www.modres.wordpress.com
- Tyndale Theological Seminary — www.tyndale.edu

Find more of Fred DeRuvo's books at the following places:

- Prophecy in the News — www.prophecyinthenews.com
- Study-Grow-Know — www.studygrowknow.com
- Amazon — www.amazon.com
- CreateSpace — www.createspace.com

www.ingramcontent.com/pod-product-compliance
Lightning Source LLC
LaVergne TN
LVHW061223100826
845148LV00004B/841

* 9 7 8 0 9 8 2 6 4 4 3 2 4 *